YOUR THOUGHTS, BODY, AND BEHAVIOR

HIGH-FUNCTIONING ANXIETY
CAN IT BE A GOOD THING?

CARDEA SIRONA

CONTENTS

INTRODUCTION

"Nothing diminishes anxiety faster than action." —Walter Anderson

That action Walter Anderson refers to in his epigraph is you reaching out for support, and choosing this book, and I'm glad you did. I'm going to help you discover the art of healing through methods I discovered and implemented into my own life that helped me deal with my own high-functioning anxiety.

The goal of my book, *Your Thoughts, Body, and Behavior*, is to help you better understand what high-functioning anxiety is and teach you helpful strategies that will help reduce your symptoms and give you a greater sense of control over your life. You will find some unique and less conventional approaches to managing anxiety along with a multitude of interactive activities to help you engage and get the best results in reducing your anxiety.

In my role as a teacher, I have faced anxiety on many levels, and I have experienced the consequences that follow. There have been times when I have witnessed colleagues, students, and friends suffering from anxiety in various forms.

I have had discussions with colleagues who suffered from anxiety as teens and learned how they spent much of their lives seeking treatment. I discovered that medication and several visits to therapists ruled their life, and as a result, they were made to believe their "illness" could only be fixed by these outside forces.

Have you been exposed to similar situations?

Were you willing to follow along in the hope of feeling normal. To gain control of your life, so as not to be a burden on your loved ones, and avoid being categorized as having a mental illness?

For most people dealing with depression and anxiety, the answers lie within themselves. Self-empowerment is one of the best tools to heal your mind, body, and soul.

You may be battling your symptoms alone, despite support from family and friends. Most of the time, it's you against your mind, which becomes your worst enemy when you're experiencing an anxiety attack.

Throughout this book, I'll be offering the solutions you will need to take control of your mind and body, unlocking the root causes, and weaknesses of anxiety disorders. As you proceed, you will learn about the connection between your mental and physical self, how outside influences can be lethal triggers, and how simple lifestyle shifts can make a huge difference when managing your condition.

Included in this book are helpful techniques to help you manage and strengthen the connection between your mind and body, as well as helping you with the following:

- Learning to focus on specific symptoms.
- Identifying the triggers.
- Learning to avoid your triggers and live a wholesome life.

- Using techniques to address both your mental and physical behavior symptoms.
- Learning the secrets to overcoming high-functioning anxiety and living a happy healthy life.

Having experienced this journey myself, and through family and friends, I'm passionate about sharing what I have learned with you.

Let me help you break free! If you are tired of dealing with the fear, the frustrations, the setbacks, and the compartments you are constantly categorized into, then I say again: Let me help you break free!

REACH OUT:
YOU ARE NOT SUFFERING ANXIETY ALONE

Did you know that one in ten people suffer from some form of mental anxiety syndrome? That is a little over 10.7% of the world's population. Shocking, isn't it? It also goes to show that you and I are not one in a million; there are many people out there who understand what we are dealing with.

According to a statistic from a 2017 study, 792 million people are estimated to suffer from some form of mental health disorder globally (Ritchie et al., 2018).

The study was based on a broad definition of mental health disorders, since the range is complex and difficult to compartmentalize. The distinctions are based on markers set by WHO's International Classification of Diseases (ICD-10), and include a range of syndromes including depression, bipolar, anxiety, schizophrenia, substance abuse, and eating disorders.

Let's not forget the number of people dealing with mental health disorders who are reluctant to seek help; therefore, these numbers are not wholly accurate or the total count. Therefore, I repeat: You are not suffering alone. You have every right to reach out for help, and admitting you need help is the first step to becoming stronger and overcoming your condition.

Here are some further findings revealed by the study:

• Anxiety disorders were identified among 284 million people globally—3.8%.

• Among that number, females make up the higher percentage.

    • Females—4.1%

    • Males—2.7%

• Depression was prevalent among 264 million of the global population—3.4%.

Statistic-wise, and from my personal experiences, anxiety-related disorders are more prevalent among women. Depression, anxiety, eating disorders, and bipolar were wider among females as well. In contrast, other mental health disorders, including those related to schizophrenia and substance abuse were greater in men, or sometimes equally distributed among the genders.

However, by no means am I gauging the severity of anxiety by gender. I had a close male friend who was diagnosed with severe anxiety, who revealed the following:

During the battle to take control of feelings, fears, and doubts that would suddenly crop up for no apparent reason, he would often end up in a very dark place—all alone. Sure, there were friends around him, who loved and cared about him—but it was like he was in a bubble all by himself, standing out of his body looking at himself and his uncontrollable rage, sadness, or despair (whatever emotion he was experiencing on heightened levels). He felt totally helpless and unable to take control.

I know the severity of dealing with high function anxiety; it's exhaustive. As an educator, I have come across students who try to hide their condition from their friends because they don't want to be labeled as "that one with the problem."

An individual diagnosed with depression or anxiety doesn't want sympathy, nor does he or she want to be perceived as different. What they need are the tools to help them take charge of their emotions, thoughts, and actions.

You're going to learn to delve deep into your mind, to discover your essence, your strengths, your weaknesses, and your breaking points.

But first, you will begin to understand the type of high-functioning anxiety you are dealing with. The easiest path to a solution is to understand the cure. Therefore, I am going to help you to understand the condition and learn how to identify your syndrome and make sense of why you've been dealing with these heightened emotions and physical weaknesses.

Acceptance Is Crucial for Initiating Change

If you have been harboring concerns or suspicions you may be suffering from some form of anxiety disorder, it is important you identify and accept any condition you may be having.

As the above statistics reveal, anxiety disorders are quite prevalent in modern society. Heightened by our busy lifestyles, we always try to adhere to the constant demand to be perfect, to prove our self-worth, and to work tirelessly even when it is not mentally or biologically possible. Simply put, we go beyond what nature intended.

If you have been made to feel that you must hide or feel ashamed of your condition, understand that that is a wrong notion.

Anxiety can overcome anyone at any time, in fact, everyone undergoes anxiety and panic attacks at some point due to various situations or reasons. Sometimes those panic attacks are due to uncompounded fear, or sudden and heightened feelings of doubt or anxiousness for no apparent reason—feelings over which you have no control.

First, accept that this is a common condition, and one that can be overcome. Anyone diagnosed as having a form of clinical depression should be aware that they are not alone and have no need to feel shame or fear.

Here are some famous people who thought on the same lines and went on to inspire and empower people like you, and me, by shouting out to the whole world that anxiety disorders do not discriminate by any category, and that anyone can be prone to the condition.

Basketball Player, Marcus Morris Sr.

A valuable player for the Los Angeles Clippers, Marcus admitted to dealing with anxiety and depression throughout his life.

Marcus grew up in Philadelphia and came from a rough neighborhood where gang violence was prevalent. In a 2018 interview with ESPN, he went on to admit that due to the rough nature of the people in his surroundings, he grew up suspicious of everyone, regardless of color or how long he knew them. Marcus and his twin brother Markieff grew up in poverty, under tough conditions, and admitted to being diagnosed with depression.

These seeds of anxiety and depression grew once he joined the National Basketball Association. Morris admits that jumping between teams left him anxious, and that he resorted to seeking solace in sleeping pills and marijuana.

Marcus Morris eventually sought help from a mental health

therapist, who he says taught him to feel calmer and happier, enabling him to become more productive (ESPN, 2018).

Singer and Actress, Ariana Grande

A bombing took place during Ariana Grande's 2017 concert at Manchester Arena. Following this, the singer started to suffer from Post-Traumatic Stress Disorder (PTSD). She went on to speak about dealing with PTSD following the bombing during a 2018 interview with British Vogue.

As well, Ariana admitted to dealing with long-term anxiety disorders throughout her life. She admits to not publicizing the syndrome and thinking that just about everyone suffered from anxiety, and so she resorted to dealing with her condition positively (Vogue, 2018).

Singer and Songwriter, Kesha

In 2017, Kesha wrote an article for *Time* on the hardships of facing the holiday season while dealing with mental illness. She admits to hitting a very low moment in life during the holidays, and how with the support of her mother, she sought help for the eating disorder she was dealing with (Time, 2017).

Kesha had previously admitted in 2016 to *Billboard* about her trials with anxiety and depression. She had this to say during her interview in 2016:

"Finding the strength to come forward about those things is not easy. But maybe, by telling my story, I can help someone else going through tough times" (Milzoff, 2016).

The above profiles are just three of the celebrities who I think are ideal for drawing inspiration from, in order to overcome the challenges that anxiety disorders place on us. Regardless of background or situation, taking charge of your condition begins with admitting you need help.

I am confident the techniques I have listed in this book will start you on the path to recovery. They are not medical treatments, but techniques and methods that have been fine-tuned by people who have and are dealing with high-functioning anxiety.

Are you ready to start healing, and take control of your life? Let's begin.

HIGH-FUNCTIONING ANXIETY

"When you change the way you look at things, the things you look at change." —Wayne Dyer

You picked up this book because you are looking for answers. You are looking for a better understanding of that diagnosis you received to make sense of why you feel the way you do.

Let's start off by helping you to understand what high-functioning anxiety really is. I'll go beyond the clinical terms for you to recognize the condition from a clear perspective. I have also included a self-assessment quiz to help you gauge yourself on a personal level against how you are dealing with symptoms related to the condition, as opposed to judging your level of high-functioning anxiety against standard markers used to diagnose anxiety.

As well, in this first chapter, we will explore the signs and symptoms that indicate you are dealing with high-functioning anxiety, in case you picked up this book based on a suspicion, and not a diagnosis.

Anxiety is a broad spectrum that is hard to diagnose from a

simple evaluation. There are various paths that lead to the development of high-functioning anxiety. Stress and worry are the main factors; such feelings stem from everyday events, feelings of nervousness, self-doubt, and fears.

The terms are often loosely used to describe one disorder, although they are all quite different and stem from various causes. High-functioning anxiety cannot be diagnosed in the same manner as phobias or panic disorders. Each condition is different and must be approached differently.

Can you recall the first time you felt an overwhelming and uncompounded fear? Or an instance when you felt extremely nervous or anxious about facing a particular situation or person? Did you experience a strong feeling of dread, anger, or even hopelessness that made you want to run away from a situation, or lash out aggressively? If you can recall instances when you felt such strong and overwhelming emotions, then these are the signs from which we can begin to diagnose your condition.

There are several tools to diagnose these conditions that are both psychological and physical, and we will explore them in this chapter.

STRESS, WORRY, AND ANXIETY:
WHAT'S THE DIFFERENCE?

How many times have people used the terms "stressed out" and "worry" in the same context?

Stress, worry, and anxiety may sound like similar problems, and they may manifest through similar symptoms, but each feeling is completely distinct from the other, and it is very important to understand the differences between each to understand the causes of high-functioning anxiety. With that being said, let's not be in a hurry to jump to a solution—instead we'll break down each condition and lay them bare so you can start to see these differences.

Define and Understand "Worry"

Worry is the word we use to describe the stresses we are under. Worry makes us reckless, scared, or aggressive. Worry can make us behave in ways we are not proud of, or it can hold us back from reaching our potential, or simply from having fun and living life to the fullest.

In short, worry is extremely tough to take control of, as it sneaks into your mind and keeps nagging at you until you become doubtful, nervous, and anxious.

Worry is, in fact, a component of anxiety. The social and emotional factors that define anxiety—or to be more specific, the cognitive characteristics of anxiety—act as a combination of thoughts and memories with negative effects that are quite often uncontrollable.

In this context, worry works on the premise of self-predictive future events. For example, consider times when you worry about an event that hasn't taken place yet. The outcome for this event is uncertain, yet you perceive it in a negative light, and believe an unfavorable outcome will no doubt take place.

Hence the uncontrollable worry, which occurs often without reason. This type of anxious worry is common among people who tend to stress over future events—ones which they have no control over. However, the severity of that worry is judged when it stems from some form of mental disorder, for example an acute phobia as a panic disorder or social phobia.

The most common disorder is Generalized Anxiety Disorder (GAD), which is diagnosed based on the person worrying uncontrollably about a range of general situations, events, outcomes, etcetera. Repeated strains of thought about oneself that are negative are often a part of worry that is related to GAD.

"I just know something bad is going to happen."
"Why do I fail at everything?"
"What if I can't do it?"

These are just a few of the negative thoughts that often dominate your mind when dealing with anxiety-related worries. GAD is far more serious than other worry-related disorders, such as social phobia. Social phobia focuses on just one type of worry—the dread of being embarrassed in public, which we all face at some point—but social phobia can become a concern when you keep expecting something embarrassing to take place.

Social phobia can stem from things like insecurity, the fear of making a mistake or being exposed, as well as becoming vulnerable to the judgment of others. Although there are memes and motivational quotes out there proclaiming "what others think of you is none of your business," for people dealing with social phobia, on a clinical level, it is not such an easy fix.

The condition can become quite unbearable when you are constantly exposed to situations that leave you vulnerable to fears of failing or looking bad in front of strangers. But a social phobia is only one aspect of worry; what if you have several worries like GAD?

The symptoms of GAD compose the type of anxiety disorder that would be described as "pathological worry," associated with deep worry or thoughts that are based on overanalyzing (rumination) situations and finding loopholes for things to go wrong.

Rumination, which is strongly linked to pathological worry, works in combination with the following:

- Overanalyzing a situation and identifying all probable causes for it to go wrong.
- Linking that pessimistic behavior to past events that cause the individual to develop low self-esteem, negative personal characteristics, and negative views of past events.

It is unclear why a person looks at a situation or event and negatively anticipates a low probability of success. In short, why do some people worry uncontrollably.

One factor is clear, though, and was identified through researching the behavior of people diagnosed with pathological worry (Hirsch & Mathews, 2012). In this research, unprecedented worry was linked to the avoidance of stressful situations from taking form, positing that such pathological worriers will go on to confirm that the condition keeps them safe, as it helps them with problem-solving. Such people dread 'uncertainty,' and will continue to worry and stress over events until their anxiety is quelled.

Worry and Anxiety Disorders: Understanding Emotional Processing

Of course, everyone experiences anxiety, whether on a pathological level or not. Quite often, the intensity of a person's emotional response to anxiety will be high or low depending on their moods, medical conditions (I, for one, tend to be irritable when suffering from flu), and the life stresses they are dealing with.

However, if you are dealing with pathological worry related to an anxiety disorder, your emotional processes are heightened, and will affect your actions, thoughts, and your perceptions.

And so, your emotional concerns or responses center on you

becoming more sensitive, as well as unconsciously more selective (stemming from your condition) toward triggers that invoke feelings of being threatened. These include:

- Worrying thoughts
- Mental images of negative outcomes
- Physical sensations

The above triggers lead to heightened levels of worry brought on by an ambiguous emotional interpretation of events, that to you seem to possess a threat. These are the emotional biases you are dealing with.

Emotional ambiguity refers to having a range of emotional responses coupled with uncertainty. Therefore, if anyone ever accuses you of "over-reacting" to a situation, that person is talking from a very shallow point of view. The level of uncertainty you have in a situation has nothing to do with "overreacting," as it is linked to a form of pathological worry you are dealing with. For you, understanding and accepting such diagnoses are key to dealing with—and healing—your condition.

Why Do You Struggle with Emotional Processing Biases

Although not conclusive, there is evidence pointing to emotional biases having genetic and environmental influences.

The low secretion of the 5-HTT gene, which is a transporter for the neurotransmitter serotonin, is said to influence negative emotional reactions, as well as a sense of vulnerability.

What Are 5-HTT Gene and Serotonin?

The 5-HTT gene is a serotonin transporter protein with links to depression, as well as autism. The gene itself is found in two forms: the long-form and the short form. People with the short form have been identified as being more prone to anxiety and depression.

Despite these findings, the gene is not actually linked to the conditions. Instead, what was common among people with the shorter 5-HTT gene was that they have smaller regions in the brain that controlled emotions—smaller in size than people who possessed the long gene.

These regions are:

- The cingulate gyrus, which is responsible for processing emotions and for regulating behavior.
- The amygdala, which generates and regulates the fear component in emotions.

It's important to understand how these two regions function so that you understand your uncompounded worry and anxiety.

The amygdala controls your response to a fearful situation, but if the fear is uncompounded, the cingulate gyrus will process those emotions and diffuse them. However, when these regions which are affected are smaller—as is the case for people with the shorter 5-HTT gene—there is a malfunction of the cingulate gyrus region, resulting in the fear going unchecked and beginning to escalate.

A fault in the cingulate gyrus can cause defects in the way you respond to certain stimuli. Such results will manifest as aggressive behavioral problems, a decrease in your emotional expressions, and even shyness.

Serotonin

The feel-good hormone, serotonin, is a chemical neurotransmitter that acts like a messenger delivering messages between the brain and nerve cells located throughout the body. Therefore, the neurotransmitter plays a part in controlling many bodily functions, including among them sleep, memory, happiness, mood, sexual desire, and the regulation of body temperature. When serotonin levels fluctuate, it can cause problems in persons psychologically. Anxiety, mania, and depression are among them.

Surprisingly, only about 10% of this neurotransmitter is produced in the brain, while a majority is produced in your gut. Gut bacteria are responsible for producing almost 90% of your serotonin levels. Serotonin is responsible for regulating your mood, happy thoughts, feelings of calmness, emotional stability, focus, and gut activity. Further conclusions have been made that tweaking the condition of your gut bacteria may be beneficial in improving mood disorders, and vice-versa. The brain can influence the quality of your gut bacteria, whereas even mild forms of stress can change the balance of your gut microbiome (the content of good and bad gut bacteria). As a result, you become more susceptible to bacteria that cause disease (Carpenter, 2012).

Can you now see the connection between reduced levels of serotonin, incessant worry, and changes in your appetite?

Serotonin and Dopamine: The Feel-Good Hormones

Sleep is another function regulated by serotonin. In this case, serotonin pairs up dopamine with another hormone neurotransmitter that is also responsible for how you feel.

Dopamine is released when we anticipate a reward, and those feelings of satisfaction we experience when we accomplish something are due to a rush of dopamine.

Dopamine acts on memory and replaying those feelings of reward to make your brain crave them again can be quite addictive, especially if you associate feelings of reward with eating. As a result, such addictions are leading causes of binge eating and obesity.

Therefore, dopamine plays a part in your decision-making function, just like serotonin. Dopamine is also responsible for the quality of your sleep and will determine its duration, all because dopamine can influence the amount of melatonin you produce.

Melatonin is what's called "the sleep hormone," and it is responsible for helping your circadian rhythm (your natural sleep-wake cycle) to stay in sync. Studies have confirmed that depriving oneself of proper sleep leads to a decrease in dopamine receptors, which can disrupt the production of melatonin, leading to sleep disorders and later anxiety syndromes.

Do you see how both serotonin and dopamine can have effects on your mental health? A disruption to your dopamine-producing system can lead to symptoms that can be diagnosed as depression. These include:

- Constantly feeling helpless.
- Having very low self-esteem.
- Losing interest in things that you were once passionate about.

Stress, trauma, and mental agony are given as probable causes for the above symptoms brought on by a dopamine disruption in your system.

Despite being linked to several symptoms, worry can be categorized into two groups.

Hypothetical Worry

This is a classic case of anxiety-related worry that is uncompounded. It simply involves you worrying unnecessarily by predicting negative outcomes of future events. Basically, hypothetical worry is brought on by events or thoughts over which you have no control. It is based on a lot of "what ifs," and can become quite unbearable.

Practical Worry

As the name suggests, this type of worry is based on daily events over which you stress. For example, meeting a deadline when you have a report to submit. This is a normal situation until you let worry stop you from completing the task, by putting it off. The number of worries eventually pile up and you end up overwhelmed and feeling helpless, dealing with the burdens you created by not dealing with the task at hand.

However, practical worry is not a simple fix of "okay, I have to get this done, so quit worrying and start doing." You could be dealing with GAD, and if so, you should understand why you're more likely to worry than complete the task.

When worry takes up most of your time, you feel exhausted, with hardly any time in which to complete your daily chores. In time, these syndromes can lead to anxiety disorders.

Here's how your worry works to cause anxiety:

Thoughts ("what if...")	Emotions	Physical Symptoms	Behavior Manifestations
	• Frustrations	• Tenseness	• Seeking distractions
	• Anxieties	• Irritability	• Postponing things
	• Worry	• Exhaustion	• Giving into distractions
	• Feeling overwhelmed	• Sleep disorders	

The above flow chart can work in a cycle to keep you in a continuous loop of overwhelming worry. Try to identify when you start to experience this sequence of events, as these are your triggers. Recognizing your triggers is the best way to stop giving into worry.

How to Manage Your Worry

1. Identify your worries. Are they within your control?
2. Did the event you were worried about take place? If it did, how did you cope, and was the outcome as bad as you had predicted?
3. Did your continuous worry about the event help to ease the situation, or did it only lead to more stress?
4. What could you have done in the moment, instead of worrying incessantly? Perhaps you can put an action plan into play. Write out what is causing your worry and see how you can deal with it.

The general idea here is to try and diffuse your uncompounded feelings of worry. Often, putting worry into perspective helps you to deal with it head-on, as you end up understanding that it was not as big a worry as your mind made it out to be.

When dealing with students who are stressed out about exams, meeting grades, and managing their time, I find that keeping a chart or diary of their events—and then adding an action plan to achieving those target—works far better than worrying and postponing things, and then letting them pile up to cause incessant worry.

Now, this is dealing with worry on a practical level, but if you are dealing with an anxiety disorder such as high-functioning anxiety, then the fix is not so easy, and requires in-depth understanding and techniques to overcome. We will get to these other disorders as we progress.

WHAT IS STRESS?

Most mental health therapists would define stress as a natural part of how we process our day-to-day activities, feelings, influences, and so on. Anyone facing life's challenges and not showing some form of stress would probably seem unnatural, right? However, most people suffering from neurodegenerative diseases, such as Alzheimer's and Parkinson's, do not feel the normal stresses of daily life, as their minds are incapable of processing such information anymore.

Our next focus will be to identify stress that leads to high-functioning anxiety, and to identify when normal stress becomes a problem.

For example, most students who transition to college life from high school must take on bigger responsibilities, the concept of being on their own, and the responsibility of doing their best when it comes to academics. These factors add burdens and stresses on the young students, who must learn to cope with them as part of acquiring a life skill.

But what happens when some of them cannot learn to cope with their stress?

Here are the signs of stress that any mental health therapist will look for:

- Worry
- Panic
- Increased heart rate
- Accelerated breathing
- Constant feelings of foreboding doom or fear
- Excessive sweating
- An inability to focus and think clearly

Having any of the above symptoms at any given time due to sudden stresses that crop up is normal. What is not normal is when these stresses are coupled with the type of pathological symptoms we discussed earlier, regarding worry. Stress caused by constant worry is a form of clinical anxiety. This type of worry-infused panic will start to affect how you function, such as by:

- Your sleep getting disrupted.
- Erratic eating habits prevailing.
- Not being able to handle normal everyday functions without feeling overwhelmed.
- In the case of students, there may be a drop in their academic performances.

Stress is your reaction to an external cause, but it becomes a problem when stress starts to affect you internally, on a mental and physical level.

How Can You Tell if You Are Dealing with Stress or Anxiety

Let's recap: Stress is your mental and physical reaction to external causes. It's a part of your natural coping mechanisms. You may deal with stress as a one-off situation (if your car breaks down on the way to an important meeting), or it may be a long-term situation, such as dealing with an illness.

Anxiety is how your mind and body deal with stress. Sometimes anxiety takes place for no reason, and you feel stressed out in situations that are not actually that bad. That kind of clinical anxiety is hard to squash and soon it starts to affect you on a physical and mental level.

Actual, physical symptoms start to manifest due to anxiety-related, unwarranted stress, including:

- You develop problems with your digestive system.
- Sleep disorders take over.
- Your fertility is affected because you develop problems with your reproductive system.
- Cardiovascular diseases become a threat.

Together with the manifestation of the above diseases, the probability of you developing a mental disease becomes very high, paving the way for you to be vulnerable to a range of anxiety disorders. Therefore, if you suspect your stress is related to anxiety, and you have not been diagnosed—or have not sought any form of help—it's good to put your overwhelming fears, stresses, and anxieties into perspective.

The following chart is designed to assist you in determining whether your feelings are due to stress, or whether they are related to anxiety.

Symptoms of Stress	Symptoms of Anxiety	Symptoms Your Stress Is Affected by Anxiety
• Happens most often because of an external reason. Exams, meeting work deadlines, your financial situation, etc. • The stress-induced by an external cause will end once the problem causing the stress is resolved. • Stress can be helpful or cause more problems. If you stress over the possibility of failing an exam; that stress makes you study harder and pass your exam with flying colors. On the other hand, stress may impact you negatively, with your worry over your exam results giving you nightmares and causing you to lose sleep, making it harder to focus on your studies. • Stress is your mind's natural coping mechanism; it can create positive or negative outcomes.	• Anxiety shows how you deal with external stress factors through internal reactions. Headaches, poor sleep, etc. • Developing anxiety because of stress keeps you in a constant loop of dread—often for no reason. You become pessimistic and apprehensive of situations, and soon those thoughts start to interfere with how you live your life. • Unlike stress that crops up due to external reasons, anxiety is an internal mental and physical syndrome that is constant—it occurs without reason. • Do you recall feeling dread, fear, and anxiety even though you were not under any danger or threat?	• You're dealing with traumatic mental and physical problems. • Headaches. • Feeling tense all the time and not knowing why. • Feelings of unease. • Body pains. • Increases in blood pressure. • Poor sleep quality.

When Stress Turns into Anxiety, You Develop the Avoidance Syndrome

When stress is affected by anxiety, it makes it difficult to function. Quite often, you end up avoiding everyday life situations because feelings of dread, doubt, and fear emerge. You may pass up applying for that promotion you deserve, or even applying for a new job. You'll start to avoid things you loved to do before, such as socializing with friends, avoiding forming new relationships, or getting together with family.

Avoidance Disorders and Their Link to Fear, Stress, and Anxiety Disorders

Avoidance behavior crops up quite often when you try to avoid dealing with stress. It is a symptom of GAD, and it is also a common behavioral response to pathological worry, as well as excessive and uncompounded fear, stress, panic, and anxiety.

Phobias, too, are quite often caused by avoidance behavior, because when you avoid facing situations and events for long, you eventually develop an aversion to such situations or events. Once that aversion takes place, even therapy may not be enough to reverse the effects.

Symptoms of Avoidance Behavior

Are you dealing with avoidance behavior due to generalized anxiety disorder? How can you tell?

Here are the symptoms:

- Hiding your emotions.
- Daydreaming or indulging in wishful thinking.
- Escapism.

- Going into self-isolation.
- Finding an excuse to avoid social gatherings, such as parties or family get-togethers.
- Often canceling plans at the last minute.
- Procrastination, and postponing actions or events.
- Avoiding certain places or going to specific places at certain times.
- Ignoring texts or calls.

If you can identify with any of the above symptoms, you could be having some form of avoidance behavior or GAD. I've found the following method a great way to get your anxieties into perspective.

Start a Journal or Diary

Processing your feelings and thoughts always become easier and clearer when you write them down and then read them back to yourself. Quite often, what you perceive in your mind is not the reality you gather when reading out those thoughts.

For example, you may have thought that people were constantly calling or texting you only to get your help, and no other reason. You might develop a syndrome where you will want to avoid interacting with false people.

Often when we process situations or engage with individuals while we are in an emotional state of distress, our perceptions are biased, as they followed our mindset at the time.

Try to Manage Your Stress and Develop Techniques to Cope

Use that same journal to manage your stress. Identify why you feel what you're feeling. Why do you want to avoid the person, situation, or event? Understanding the root cause of your avoidance behavior is the first step in finding a solution and developing coping skills for those emotions that threaten to take over your life.

First, ask yourself if the trigger or situation that caused your avoidance behavior could have been avoided. Think about a solution. Don't allow yourself to let this situation rule your life. Ask yourself the all-important question, "what can I do?" Doing this is going to stimulate your mind to bring about a solution. Think of it this way: You are giving your mind a command to find a solution, instead of giving in to the negative emotion which tells your mind that the negative emotion is justified.

Next, let's look at anxiety, which as you would have gathered by now, is what both heightened worry and stress evolve into. Anxiety is not easy to categorize, as it takes many forms and has many different symptoms. To put it in a lighter vein, analyzing anxiety is enough to cause you anxiety!

WHAT IS ANXIETY?

Anxiety develops as a response to stress or worry. It is a physical manifestation caused by exterior triggers. And just like we already established that worry and stress are a part of your natural coping mechanisms, anxiety, too, is a natural reflex to external distressing factors. Anxiety can quickly become a mental health disorder when coupled with acute stress and pathological worry, among other factors. Extreme anxiety that is long-term and starts to interfere with your normal lifestyle will manifest in a range of different illnesses, which is why anxiety disorders are among the highest mental health disorders in the US.

a fact that will stun you (ADAA, 2021):

- Most anxiety disorders can be treated successfully, but only 36.9% of people dealing with the condition will seek help.
- The probability of people dealing with an anxiety disorder having to pay frequent visits to the doctor is three to five. Such people are six times more likely to be diagnosed and admitted to the hospital with a psychiatric disorder.

We know that stress and worry are caused by external factors, and that anxiety occurs as physical symptoms, but what are the biological changes that cause these physical symptoms to occur?

- Brain chemistry
- Genetics
- A person's personality
- Life situations

Often, depression is diagnosed among people with an anxiety disorder, with about half of those people having some form of depression to deal with as well.

Common Types of Anxiety Disorder Prevalent in Our Society

- Generalized Anxiety Disorder (GAD). 3.1% of the US population deal with GAD. That is 6.8 million adults, of which only 43.2% are receiving treatment.
- Panic Disorder (PD) affects six million adults, which is 2.7% of the US population.
- Social Anxiety Disorders (SAD) affect 6.8% of the population, which is 15 million adults. SAD begins early, at around age 13.

- Post-Traumatic Stress Disorder affects 7.7 million adults, which is 3.5% of the population. Sexual assault and or rape are the likeliest causes of PTSD, while childhood sexual abuse is a trigger for developing PTSD in adulthood.

Children between the ages of 13–18 are candidates for developing anxiety-related disorders, and when left untreated, can lead to them developing destructive habits such as substance abuse and social distancing, as well as lack of interest in academic work.

How to Identify Anxiety

Symptoms of anxiety are no different from what you experience when dealing with stress-related anxiety. Differences will depend on the individual. Just like the variety of anxiety disorders diagnosed to date, symptoms, too, will change from person to person. These include:

- Butterflies in the stomach
- Having an out-of-body experience
- Heart palpitations
- Loss of concentrations
- Shortness of breath or heightened breathing
- Insomnia

How Do I Identify an Anxiety Attack

Several emotions come into play when a person is experiencing an anxiety attack. An overwhelming feeling of unease or nervousness takes over, together with worry, fear, or feeling distress. An anxiety attack does not occur instantly; it builds over a course of time and will heighten as the event, reason, or person causing the anxiety draws near. Not everyone experiences the same type of anxiety attacks; they will keep changing from time to time, and from person to person. Therefore, symptoms you have experienced before could suddenly change to a different set of emotions.

Here are some of the physical symptoms you may experience during an anxiety attack:

- Excessive sweating
- Dry mouth
- Sudden hot flashes or chills
- Uncontrollable feelings of distress
- Feeling restless
- Experiencing acute fear
- Tingling or a numbing sensation

How Do I Determine if I Am Dealing with Anxiety

Anyone experiencing symptoms of anxiety, or anyone who suspects they may be borderline, should seek the help of a qualified mental health therapist—a psychologist, a psychiatrist, or a clinical social worker. The diagnosis will consist of a physical exam, including a blood test to determine if you are dealing with hypothyroidism, as the condition could also contribute to the emotions or physical symptoms you are feeling.

Your medication history will also be checked, as certain prescription drugs taken for diseases such as Parkinson's or Arthritis can cause anxiety-related symptoms. As well as a psychological evaluation will follow, where your family history is checked, with an emphasis placed on the possibility of anxiety-related diseases being a part of your family history.

Is It Possible to Deal with Anxiety-Related Diseases Naturally

There are several methods used to deal with anxiety that are not related to prescription medication, scientific therapies, or treatment plans.

The natural remedies are, in fact, based on simple lifestyle changes, most of which will be covered in more detail in upcoming chapters, but will consist of the following:

• Changes in the diet and eating healthier food.

• Improving nightly sleep quality by striving for at least eight hours of quality sleep.

• Cultivating an active lifestyle that stimulates your mind and offers you physical activity to improve overall mind and body revitalization.

• Simple tweaks such as avoiding alcohol and smoking.

   • Alcohol affects serotonin and the production of other neurotransmitters in the brain, by reducing their levels. Due to the reduced levels of mood controlling hormones your anxiety can worsen after the effects of alcohol wear off. They remain on that heightened level for many hours until the hormone levels are regularized again. Some people turn to alcohol as a tool to cope with anxiety, but they end up heightening the condition.
   • Alcohol has a distressing effect on the amygdala, which if you recall, is the part of your brain that regulates your response to fear and other negative emotions.
   • Smoking, which is often practiced as a method of

easing one's stress and anxiety, has quite the opposite effect on anxiety-related syndromes. This is, notably, apart from the grave physical ill-health that occurs as a result of smoking.

• Smoking is common in people suffering with depression. It is linked to fluctuating levels of dopamine, and people with depression exhibit low levels of dopamine. The nicotine in cigarettes stimulates the brain to produce more dopamine, thus rewarding you with that feel-good sensation. And while you may think this is a good sign, hold on before you reach for that cigarette! Since nicotine induces a dopamine release, the brain soon stops its own natural process of responding to its stimulants to release dopamine. And so, your dopamine levels drop, resulting in you smoking more, and associating smoking with that reward sensations, making it impossible to quit.

• If becoming an unwitting addict is not enough to convince you that smoking is bad, do some research on the many health hazards that are caused by nicotine, tar, and cyanide, which are present in cigarette smoke.

• Avoiding or reducing the consumption of caffeine.

Simple lifestyle changes are very effective and powerful tools for dealing with anxiety, slowing its progress, and even preventing simple stresses and fears from growing into clinical anxiety. In fact, medical practitioners recommend a component of lifestyle changes as mentioned above to successfully treat anxiety disorders, together with prescription medication.

As we move on to our next topic, which is discovering specifically what high-functioning anxiety is, it is important to keep in mind the power of self-healing. Self-healing can be achieved through following the techniques and lifestyle changes I will be introducing you to.

WHAT IS HIGH-FUNCTIONING ANXIETY?

Our modern lifestyles are stressful, highly demanding, and can easily lead to worry, fear, and a great deal of stress. It is my goal, however, to help you rediscover the joy of those good moments in life, which make life worthwhile.

As we have already established, fear, worry, and stress can lead to anxiety, and anxiety is quite complicated, manifesting itself as different conditions with a variety of symptoms. Most anxiety-related syndromes will change how you function, cause a disruption to your daily routine, and put a stop to your activities, causing you to retreat into a world of your own.

However, there are instances where a person is suffering stress, fear, and doubt related to anxiety without the manifestation of physical and mental symptoms. This is what high-functioning anxiety is: It is not a formally diagnosed medical condition, and it is not listed in the Diagnostic and Statistical Manual of Mental Disorders (DSM-5) in which close to 70 disorders are listed, but high-functioning anxiety is very real and causes serious damage in the long run. Sadly, people on the outside do not see this anxiety in their friends, colleagues, or loved ones before it's too late, because people dealing with high-functioning anxiety disorder are experts at hiding their tribulations, emotions, and insecurities.

I have encountered individuals with high-functioning anxiety who never displayed any of the symptoms we discussed under anxiety, stress, and worry. The syndrome can affect anyone; high-achieving students or the teacher who seems to have everything going for them. Such people can manage their lives and face challenges successfully, but that is not who they are internally.

People suffering from high-functioning anxiety will seem outwardly normal and perfectly capable of taking care of themselves. They can be fortunate in life and seem to 'have it all' in terms of success, friends, relationships. However, they are actually dealing with stress, fear, doubt, anxiety, and harmful obsessive thoughts.

How to Identify Symptoms of High-functioning Anxiety

Research into high-functioning anxiety is limited since it hasn't been officially diagnosed, making it difficult to identify symptoms. And since those dealing with the condition are experts at masking their inner turmoil, it is quite difficult to analyze.

Yet, most anxiety disorder health experts claim the symptoms are very similar to generalized anxiety disorder (GAD).

Some of the GAD symptoms that trickle over to high-functioning anxiety, which are noticeable and may prompt someone to seek a solution include the following:

- Anxiety and worry that lasts for more than six months.
- Feelings of stress because of feeling on edge.
- Headaches brought on by constant jaw clenching.
- Difficulty in focusing.
- Bad moods, grumpiness, and frequent irritability.
- Increased feeling of restlessness.
- Suffering from sleep disorders such as insomnia.
- Tense muscles and bodily aches.
- Stoop or hunched shoulders.

Do you find yourself in a constant angry or snappy mood, especially when you are busy? Do you hate dealing with constant headaches?

Do you find it difficult to fall asleep, or do you wake up more tired than before you went to bed? Do you attribute that feeling of fatigue to poor sleep quality where you are unable to sleep for long stretches of time, or achieve deep sleep?

The easiest way to understand this two-faced syndrome is to think of high-functioning anxiety as having a good and a bad side. The good side is the fact that you can function normally, carry out your daily life tasks, and enjoy a good level of success in your career, schoolwork, and life in general.

The bad side is despite the mask of goodness, there is a festering soul concealed behind it, which is like a ticking time bomb. Your inner struggles are hidden, and because you are outwardly successful, you are reluctant to cry out for help. Despite living a lie, you feel obliged to keep up the charade and suffer in silence. Therefore, no one can come to your rescue, as your outward portrayal is one of success with an "I've got it all together" attitude.

This is a very sad reality, and no one deserves to deal with the painful symptoms of high-functioning anxiety all alone.

How to Determine if You Are Dealing with High-functioning Anxiety, and the Causes, and Healing Methods Available

If you are dealing with high-functioning anxiety while managing your daily tasks—without so much as a hint of the internal trauma you are bearing up—you may be confused about why you are feeling the way you are, especially when everything else in your life seems to be on course.

If you are dealing with high-functioning anxiety while simply trying to live your life, then you are most likely hiding your internal trauma from the people you interact with daily. As you keep up this facade, you may be confused as to why your exterior life seems so normal, while your interior one feels like a perpetual crisis.

You may feel alone; unable to reach out to family and friends who see you as nothing but successful and happy. However, like all other anxiety disorders, this burden is not yours to bear alone. Just like keeping a journal can help you put stress and worry into perspective, writing down the actual feelings you feel is a good way to start accepting the reality of the condition your mind is bearing the weight of. Keeping your feelings hidden only adds to an increase of the condition and stops you from healing —even if you want to. Therefore, acknowledging your troubles and emotional turmoil is how you can begin to heal through the remedies and techniques I am going to suggest in the next few chapters. High-functioning anxiety is highly treatable, once you're able to move on and start enjoying a life free from the burdens you are dealing with currently. Healing is a step-by-step process, and once you start the action of taking charge of your condition, you are going to start experiencing drastic improvements.

What Causes High-functioning Anxiety to Occur

High-functioning anxiety can be defined as an internal struggle made up of the fears, stresses, and worries that are always present in your mind. Environmental factors can be a very probable source of this, especially when influenced by your busy lifestyle. Your background can also provide answers to why you are dealing with the uncontrollable fears and doubts that are a part of the disorder. They could be due to a past traumatic event in your life.

The other cause is genetics, as your genes could be responsible for you inheriting the condition. Based on these factors, let's look at some of the identified causes of high-functioning anxiety:

- Genetics. Genetics can play a role when you come from a family with a history of anxiety disorders. Your

parents or nearest relatives having a history of
disorders are more likely to cause your anxiety than a
distant relative. What researchers have discovered is
that a combination of genes—and not a single gene—
is responsible for passing down related conditions, as
well as depression. A good sign of anxiety being a part
of your family background is someone developing it at
a very young age. Dealing with this below the age of
20 is the most probable reason to think your
condition is hereditary.

- A traumatic event in your past. Becoming exposed to
  sudden trauma in your childhood or in your recent
  past can be the root cause of your high-functioning
  anxiety disorder. Such an event can include becoming
  exposed to a violent event through experience, or as a
  witness. This can involve having to deal with the
  unanticipated loss of a loved one, being a part of
  communal riots and or wars, and facing natural
  disasters.

- Dealing with a demanding and very stressful lifestyle.
  This could be your job, your family life in which you
  are the sole breadwinner or the primary caretaker or
  having to juggle several responsibilities at the same
  time.

- Being a student. A student having to meet high
  expectations and demands from their family can cause
  anxiety. Even your own standards that make you push
  yourself beyond your comfort zone will lead to high-
  functioning anxiety, which makes you miserable
  internally, while outwardly you are still capable of
  meeting all your goals. I've come across many
  students who have very high standards and ambitions
  set by themselves. They often end up burning out, as
  they try to meet those goals and not accept their

limitations. Often, to do our best, we need to take a break, decompress, and rejuvenate. Pushing yourself to constantly strive for perfection is a huge burden to bear for you mentally and physically.

- Shyness. This can stem from childhood, and can also cause high-functioning anxiety, where the person is withdrawn and less likely to let their emotions show. As a result, they may develop a condition where they learn to hide what they are feeling internally.
- Dealing with long-term financial problems. This can include stressful legal matters.
- Extreme loneliness is also a cause of high-functioning anxiety. Loneliness can be masked by the outside world. For example, social media platforms such as Instagram and Facebook, where a person's projected image is wholly different from what they are dealing with internally, prevents family or friends from catching on to the loneliness, sadness, or anxiety the individual is facing.

YouTubers and Instagram influencers are prime examples of the pressure and anxiety of keeping up an image that is perceived as perfect from the outside but troubled internally.

Another example of this is Olivia Culpo, who has admitted that maintaining a 'perfect' Instagram persona through updates of her idyllic lifestyle had contributed to masking all that she had been suffering internally. She went on to claim that at the height of her depression, she was struggling with excessive smoking and drinking, as well as appetite loss, all the while keeping up appearances on social media that made her look happy and put together externally (Culpo, 2019).

Many popular vloggers like Lily Singh, Elle Mills, and Zoella have announced at one point or another that they need a break from their respective platforms and personas, which is the first step to healing—acknowledging you need to fix your emotions.

- Abuse in childhood. This is a trigger for harboring the stresses of high-functioning anxiety. Sexual, physical, and mental abuse are all causes.
- Medical conditions. These can include thyroid issues, which can cause the symptoms you are dealing with. Diseases linked to the malfunction of your thyroid gland can cause anxiety and depression to surface together with mood alterations. The thyroid is a small gland found at the base of your neck that is shaped like a butterfly.

The thyroid makes the T3 and T4 hormones, which control your metabolism by telling your body how much energy to expend. A dysfunction of this gland, therefore, leads to many complications, among which anxiety symptoms are some.

Hyperthyroidism is caused by an overactive thyroid gland, and symptoms include the following:

- Irritability
- Nervousness
- Restlessness
- Anxiety

Hypothyroidism is caused by an underactive thyroid gland with symptoms of:

- Depression
- Fatigue that is mild or very severe

SIGNS AND SYMPTOMS OF HIGH-FUNCTIONING ANXIETY DISORDER

High-functioning anxiety is a condition that does not seem like a condition—externally or internally—because the individual dealing with it will often not associate the emotions with anxiety.

As mentioned previously, as it is not recognized as a mental disorder, how do you even acknowledge you are dealing with it? The physical symptoms are certainly hard to spot.

- Typical physical symptoms associated with the other anxiety disorder are not present. Difficulty functioning with daily tasks, lethargy, avoidance disorders, etcetera, are not symptoms associated with high-functioning anxiety. Heart palpitations which increase breathing and butterflies in the stomach may be present, but not as heightened as other anxiety disorders that are taken as a cause for concern.
- Some symptoms that are noticeable will be diagnosed as depression with high-functioning anxiety going unnoticed.

Let's look at some common symptoms that work in combination to indicate that you are dealing with high-functioning anxiety.

The following chart will help you to understand how the outward symptoms correlate with the inward struggles of a person with high-functioning anxiety.

Outward Symptoms	Inward Struggles
• No sign to be suffering from any form of anxiety • No stress • No worry • Is a perfectionist • Has a Type-A personality (high achiever, very competitive and impatient) • Climbs the corporate ladder • Productive and proactive • Positive attitude • Outgoing personality • Overachiever • Appears to have a calm demeanor • Is level-headed • Stickler for detail • Well organized • Appears to have their life in order	• Experiences shortness of breath, excessive sweating, and gets the shakes • Suffers from frequent diarrhea and must urinate continually • Feels exhausted • Endures feeling panic internally • Has muscle weakness and tension • Suffers from feeling dizzy • Heart races from time to time • Insomnia or other sleep disorders • Body temperature is irregular • Suffers from unsettling thoughts that scare them

The Impact of Not Treating High-functioning Anxiety

Left untreated, high-functioning anxiety will lead to depression, which is sadly the stage at which most individuals decide to seek help. That is not all; however, the condition, which is not considered an illness, will cause diagnosed mental health problems as well as other physical problems. Therefore, you are at a high risk of developing the following:

- Depression, the most likely syndrome high-functioning anxiety evolves into.
- Substance abuse, i.e., alcohol and drugs.
- Developing chronic diseases, such as heart ailments, gastrointestinal diseases, irritable bowel syndrome (IBS), asthma, stroke, chronic obstructive pulmonary disease (COPD), and functional dyspepsia, which is a type of chronic indigestion.

Left untreated, high-functioning anxiety can lead to life-threatening situations and even shorten a person's lifespan.

The Link Between High-functioning Anxiety and Depression

Anxiety and depression often coexist because anxiety, when left untreated, leads to depression. Experiments conducted on people diagnosed with depression proved that over 50% of them were also dealing with a high level of anxiety. The diagnosis was "anxious depression," the term given to a Major Depressive Disorder (MDD), which is combined with depression and high levels of anxiety (Anxious Depression, 2021).

While having positive symptoms outwardly, high-functioning anxiety can soon turn dark when it leads to depression. When that happens, your symptoms are no longer shrouded in secrecy, it gets harder to simply get out of bed each day. In addition, you are no longer passionate about things you love to do, you perceive your life as worthless, and you develop insomnia and other related sleep disorders.

Likewise, there are instances when depression works to create high-functioning anxiety, making it highly valuable to seek treatment for any form of mental condition you suspect you are dealing with.

Treatment for High-functioning Anxiety

The traditional form of treatment for high-functioning anxiety is the same as for other anxiety diseases. Prescription medication, therapy, or a combination of both is commonly recommended.

Cognitive Behavioral Therapy (CBT)

CBT is a frequently used form of therapy that helps the patients heal by changing their mindset, or rather the way they think. By changing their thinking patterns, they will be able to better understand their condition, as well as the behavior patterns that are linked to it.This invariably opens their eyes to the misrepresentations in their behavior and thoughts which they have been maintaining for so long.

Talk Therapy

One form of natural therapy that is proving to be successful is talk therapy, where the patient—as you can imagine—talks to the therapist about their internal struggles. Talking about those struggles makes them real, unmasking them as a result, and making it easier to admit their vulnerabilities.

Prescription Medication

Prescription medicine can include several types of medicines: antidepressants, beta-blockers, benzodiazepines, and selective serotonin reuptake inhibitors (SSRIs).

Below is a simple quiz you can take to evaluate your emotions, stresses, and physical symptoms to determine if you are vulnerable to being diagnosed as having anxiety.

Interactive Tool for a Casual Self-Assessment of Anxiety

Use this quiz to determine if you are dealing with any form of anxiety disorder. The questions and answers are based on various symptoms and their severity for GAD. This quiz is by no means a finalized diagnosis of whether you are having anxiety or not but should be enough for you to understand and make sense of some of the stresses and worries you have been dealing with.

Give yourself a score of 0–3 depending on the type of answer you choose. Write down each mark you receive because you must add it up at the end.

How Many Times in the Past Month Have You Had to Deal with the Following Emotional and Physical Symptoms?	Never	Occasionally, on Some Days	At Least for Half the Time	Practically Every Day	Score
1. Worry seems to constantly take over your emotions and you find yourself agonizing over random unimportant matters.	0	1	2	3	
2. You have been feeling anxious or nervous without reason and it has made you jittery and unsure of yourself.	0	1	2	3	
3. Your worry is out of control, you are aware of it but unable to do anything to stop it.	0	1	2	3	
4. You are increasingly restless and often feel impatient.	0	1	2	3	
5. You try to relax, but you can't.	0	1	2	3	

How Many Times in the Past Month Have You Had to Deal with the Following Emotional and Physical Symptoms?	Never	Occasionally, on Some Days	At Least for Half the Time	Practically Every Day	Score
6. Feelings of doom are invading your mind and you expect bad news or a calamity to happen, but you have no solid reason for these feelings.	0	1	2	3	
7. You snap at people around you and lose your temper.	0	1	2	3	
Total score for each column					

Score Guide to Determine Your Probable Anxiety Level

- 0–4 = low anxiety level
- 5–9 = medium anxiety level
- 10–14= medium to high anxiety
- 15–21 = very high anxiety

A score of more than 10 may require a proper evaluation of your mental health situation, to determine your level of anxiety and if you could be suffering from high-functioning anxiety or another form of anxiety disorder.

In the next chapter, I'll delve deeper into the natural healing process of high-functioning anxiety. We will use the anxiety triangle to decipher each emotion, thought, and behavior trend to help you make sense of your unsettled thoughts, as well as to show you the connection between your mind, thoughts, and behavior.

2

THE ANXIETY TRIANGLE

"Man is not worried by real problems so much as by his imagined anxieties about real problems." —Epictetus

Welcome to Chapter 2, where your process of healing begins!

Here, I will introduce you to the anxiety triangle, which is the connection between your thoughts, body, and behavior. In doing so, you will learn how anxiety controls your reactions to events, situations, and people you find distressing, dangerous, or fearful.

You will also learn how the anxiety triangle can save you from a dangerous situation and how it puts into action that sudden fight or flight decision you make. Understanding the process is a very crucial link to understanding your anxiety and why you are dealing with all those emotions. Ultimately, you will learn how to take control of them.

We will use the points you learned in the previous chapter to link your behavior and battle with high-functioning anxiety— and morph them into a simple process involving the anxiety triangle taking you on the wrong path due to genetics, your present lifestyle habits, or a past traumatic event.

The very fact that you could be harboring a Type-A personality is cause for concern when dissecting your high-functioning anxiety symptoms. What exactly is a Type-A personality? We commonly learn of type-A people as being go-getters, and as easily irritable people but let me help you assess where your personality stands in that context. Let's see where you can make simple changes in your thoughts and behavior to help ease your situation and lower your anxiety levels. Sometimes all it takes are some simple tweaks, just like when you reboot your computer or restart your phone if the system gets 'stuck.'

SELF-AWARENESS AND TAKING CONTROL OF YOUR THOUGHTS ON THE ANXIETY TRIANGLE

The anxiety triangle, also called the cognitive triangle, works according to two theories: Creating self-awareness, and learning to think about what you are thinking (your thoughts). The word for the latter theory is "metacognition."

I find metacognition wholly fascinating because it makes us think about what we are thinking. This is a marvelous concept really, as it solves a lot of problems, misunderstandings, and arguments. While I may be dreaming up a theory to use metacognition to bring about world peace someday, let's, get down to the business at hand, which is helping you to get a grasp of your high-functioning anxiety.

The anxiety triangle uses the two factors—metacognition and self-awareness—to help you start taking control of your thoughts, emotions, and behavior, which for you right now, may feel as though they have a mind of their own.

Top Point of the Triangle—Negative Thoughts

We will be using the three points of the triangle to under-stand your thoughts, emotions, and behavior. Let's start with the top of the triangle; the upper point which represents your negative thoughts.

Thoughts in this context refer to that auto reflex you possess of evaluation, where you gauge your self-worth on a pre-set conception of who you are. Therefore, your thoughts will be on a loop, repeating the same message back to you. And when it comes to high-functioning anxiety, those thoughts are not very nice—in fact, they are downright nasty.

It's important to understand that negative thoughts of putting yourself down—self-criticism, those thoughts have been around not today, yesterday, or last week; they are well-settled in your mind, and they are toxic. They are your low self-esteem, wherein you have categorized yourself into a box in which you tell yourself that just about anything can go wrong with what you are about to do. The "what ifs" and "I don't think I can."

Such thoughts are extremely difficult to grasp, but you can make them real, thus giving yourself no option but to acknowl-edge them. To make them real, you must identify them, and I find that sitting down and writing out every one of those nega-tive thoughts helps to put them into their own box.

I asked some of my colleagues and students who suspected they were dealing with high-functioning anxiety to write down their negative thoughts. For each of those negative thoughts, I asked them to provide a topic, so that we could categorize them easily. We came up with a very interesting list. Let's see how many of these negative thoughts you can identify with.

Your Auto Thought Structure

- Thoughts that generalize negative conclusions. You envision a negative outcome for every event (there is no seeing the 'bright side' here). This kind of thinking happens when you are constantly reminding yourself of the one time when things didn't work out the way you planned. You then apply that negative experience to all other experiences or events in your life, thinking they too, are going to fail. This results in generalized thoughts of failure for everything you do. We jokingly call some people 'killjoys,' without realizing the battles they may be dealing with.
- Thoughts that only recognize success. You are a winner, or you are a total failure. People who listed these negative thoughts told me that they failed to form a compromise in what they did. This necessitated that they had to succeed at everything, or else they saw themselves as failures. It was a simple uncompromised thinking pattern.
- Thoughts that conclude in negativity. Negative decisions every time. This thought has you jumping to conclusions that are always negative, whether you have the facts straight or not.
- Thoughts that shun positivity. Positive thoughts or decisions are dismissed or discouraged because it is easier for you to see everything negatively. Therefore, you dismiss any positive thoughts or suggestions that are put your way, even justifying your decision by connecting them to negative experiences you have had. You even go so far as to think you know what the other person is thinking, and that it is a negative thought about you! You become so unreasonable that

you refuse to see otherwise and embrace that festering thought of negativity.

- Thoughts that exaggerate to demean. Making a mountain out of a molehill. You automatically make a big deal out of your failures, or you overpraise another's achievements. Conversely, for example, you make things appear much smaller in perspective than they are, which downplays your achievements as not being important.
- Thoughts that put you down. Attaching labels to yourself. This is a very damaging type of thought which can harm your self-esteem. "I am never going to be good enough", or "why am I such a loser?" are examples of such thoughts.
- Thoughts that are always governed by your negative emotions. Reflecting those negative emotions in your thoughts and decisions. For example, your friends ask you to join them on a weekend getaway to the beach. They tell you about how much fun it will be for you all to spend time together in the sun and surf. But despite the evidence of all factors being in favor of the trip (weather, everyone's availability, and so on), your emotions tell you that you will only feel out of place, disappointed, and even sad. And so, you let your negative emotions rule and you think "I will be in the way," or "I won't have fun," and you decline to join your friends on the trip. See how those negative emotions influenced your thoughts to become negative too?
- Thoughts that make you take on the blame. Whether or not you are directly responsible for external events with bad outcomes, your thoughts will lead you to take responsibility.

How many of the above topics can you identify with?

It is these negative thoughts that make up the tip of the triangle and acknowledging them is the first step toward dissecting and disapproving those things that have been burdening you for years. Write them down and put them into perspective, so you can see how most of those thoughts really do not make sense or hold sway with who you really are.

Bottom Point One of the Triangle—Emotions

This point represents your emotions. The negative emotions represented in the anxiety triangle are different from thoughts because they are straightforward. Where a thought will have you thinking something along the lines of "you are stressing me out," your emotion would have you saying, "I am angry." The emotion, therefore, is anger.

Also, anger happens to be one of the most common emotions that people with high-functioning anxiety seem to be able to identify with. This is because it stays within the parameters of hiding your true emotions, which is what people with this type of anxiety do. Therefore, anger is an excellent mask to hide hurt, sadness, disappointment, etcetera. Anger does not showcase how vulnerable you really are, internally.

To start healing and finding a solution to the negative emotions that make up this point of the triangle, you must start experimenting with different labels for your emotions. Labels that will make you more vulnerable and open to 'softer' ones, which will help you to connect with friends and family—who, in turn, will help you heal. In doing so, you will be 'easing' the burden of your high-functioning anxiety by not having to keep it hidden all the time.

Discover the Real Emotions Behind Your High-functioning Anxiety

The more you explore your feelings, the more you will discover the *true* emotions behind them.

- If a strong emotion takes you over, such as anger, try identifying the *real* emotion you are experiencing at that moment.

For example, you may get angry about your colleague getting the promotion you worked so hard for, but when analyzed, what you are really feeling is disappointment for being let down, and sadness that your hard work was not recognized. If it helps, write down that underlying emotion.

- Once you identify that true feeling, try to observe how your emotional mood changes. Does the identity of the new emotion make it easier for you to process your thoughts?

Does it make you feel more vulnerable?

When you found out you didn't get the promotion, you felt angry, but when you explored what you were really feeling, the situation became easier to deal with. It made you vulnerable, but you were open to accepting your feelings of disappointment, which cleared the confusion and the mental block you would otherwise be carrying around.

Becoming vulnerable to life's situations is what makes us stronger emotionally. Hiding behind a strong emotion like anger only suppresses your true feelings and increases your levels of anxiety. It's like crying; often a good cry over something that was bothering us tends to fix the way we feel, simply because we gave into that emotion.

Give in to your true emotions so your mind can process events better, without leaving you to deal with the burden of unaddressed issues.

- Writing down your feelings is a good method to let those hidden emotions flow, and it will help to alleviate the stress in your mind. You'll be surprised how easily you can tune into your softer emotions once you let go of the aggressive ones.

Bottom Point Two of the Anxiety Triangle—Behavior

The third point is, of course, behavior—which is an amalgamation of your feelings and your conduct. You must learn that by simply changing your thoughts and your emotions, you are able to change your behavior. Conversely, you can manipulate your behavior to change your feelings and your conduct—that is, your emotions and your thoughts.

As an example, you must attend a family gathering, but your emotions tell you that you will not enjoy it. Your thoughts seal the deal, by saying "going to this dinner is going to upset my mood." But if you force yourself to go to dinner, your emotions and thoughts are going to change.

Both are going to think, "okay, so we are going to this dinner; let's try to make the most of it." Your emotions will say "I feel happy," and your thoughts will follow up with "I get to taste mom's beef stew and take some home, so I am happy I came."

Although you may have felt anxious about attending a social event, and being around a lot of people, by forcing yourself to go you ended up finding distractions that deterred you from thinking about your anxieties, which is a good thing. What you must do is build the courage to work on using your behavior to override certain aspects of your high-functioning anxiety, which is linked to your emotions and thoughts.

This, of course, isn't easy, and your thoughts and emotions are not going to engage in a happy dialogue as I have given in the example above. But it is possible, and that is the fact you cling to so that you can pull yourself out of your high-functioning anxiety before it turns clinical and transitions into depression.

Can you now see the connection between your thoughts, emotions, and behavior?

Each can be turned around to influence the other, which means you have several methods of dealing with your anxiety issues.

It is not a case of controlling your emotions to avoid anxiety; neither is it a case of watching your behavior or being mindful of your thoughts. It's all three in combination and each one can be used to influence the other.

The chart shows how all three factors intertwine with one another, and by controlling one factor you can change how your anxiety affects your day-to-day life.

Thoughts
↑↓
Emotions
↑↓
Behavior

Next, let's look at the connection between your mind and body, and how your mind is powerful enough to influence your body.

UNDERSTANDING THE CONNECTION BETWEEN YOUR MIND AND BODY—TAKE CHARGE OF YOUR ANXIETY

The way you think and feel, which is your emotional state, can directly influence your physical health. Conversely, there are many factors that can influence your emotional state causing stress, fear, worry, sadness, and anxiety, all of which at times will manifest as physical symptoms from your body, making you ill.

If you are dealing with a lot of stress at your workplace, it is likely that this stress and worry will manifest as high blood pressure, obesity, diabetes, heart palpitations, difficulty in breathing, and even stress ulcers in the stomach. It is important to note that stress ulcers are very different from normal peptic ulcers.

Erosion of the stomach's lining is what is called an ulcer and sometimes due to stress, anxiety, and other mental trauma. The ulcer takes place due to trauma-induced increase of stomach acids or disruptions in the circulatory system, among other factors. As you can see, the link between the mind and body is quite clear.

High-functioning Anxiety and the Mind

As we discussed previously, high-functioning anxiety develops from past traumas, environmental pressure, or genetics; all these factors come from the mind, which means your high-functioning anxiety is also influenced by the mind.

As an example, let's assume that you may be wildly successful in your life, despite masking your inner turmoil while battling high-functioning anxiety.

Still, you justify your late nights at the office as clearing the path for more future promotions, along with a chance for you to outdo your colleagues and make CEO.

But, on the flip side, you are probably very irritable; you snap at your family members, your colleagues, and perhaps the taxi driver for taking a route you disapproved of. On top of this, you are also harboring a battle against type 2 diabetes, where your blood sugar levels fluctuate quite randomly.

The person I described; ignores the signals their mind is sending them through their body. The failure to make this connection, slow down, and pay attention to their emotions could lead to depression or other anxiety disorders if they do not learn to relax and reduce stress.

Let me remind you about the anxiety triangle and the point representing emotions, and how important it is to feel your *true* emotions, because if you do not, they manifest as ailments through your body, ushering in depression and anxiety.

The Emotional Biochemistry

It is important to remember that your gut microbiome is connected to your serotonin levels. Your gut microbiome is responsible for manufacturing close to 90% of your serotonin supply. Serotonin governs your emotions and works closely with the 5-HTT gene, as mentioned previously in Chapter 1.

Emotions, therefore, share a close link to the chemical processes (biochemistry) in your body. Your biochemistry is linked to your digestive system, your nervous system, your endocrine (the collection of glands that secrete your hormones), and your immune system. This connection confirms that your emotional and mental stimuli (which are your normal emotions and thoughts) are not just linked to brain activity but come from various parts of your body. All these feelings, both emotional and physical, are interconnected and can influence each other.

High-functioning anxiety is not a medically diagnosed

illness; the symptoms are not as severe as diagnosed anxiety disorders and depression. But the condition can develop into depression, which is a serious mental illness with strong enough symptoms to warrant medical treatment.

Therefore, is high-functioning anxiety in part an imaginary illness? A psychosomatic, perhaps?

Psychosomatic refers to the connection between the mind and body, and there is increasing evidence that these two have a strong influence on one another. Researchers are now acknowledging that our emotions and thoughts possess the power to both heal our bodies or make them sick.

This theory makes high-functioning anxiety a very *real* illness, but one that can be conquered through thoughts, emotions, and behavior. However, I am not discouraging you from getting a medical diagnosis for your condition—this is because, until facts are checked and conclusions are made professionally, one cannot play guessing games with the mind.

Meditation and the Immunity Emotional Link—Addressing the Mind

Several studies have been conducted among groups of people to prove the theory of meditation and its power over the immune system. Those who followed a mindfulness meditation program showed the following results (Black & Slavich, 2016):

- The anterior brain activity (left side) of the subjects who followed the meditation course had improved. An increase in left side brain activity signifies feelings of positivity.
- Another significant plus for the group that followed the meditation program was the development of stronger antibodies than average, in a response to flu shots.

- The study concluded that meditation-induced strengthening of the left side anterior brain activity had a direct link to a stronger immune system.

Learn to Calm Your Mind and Body

The above study proves that simple fixes work to both improve the positive response of your brain and bump up your immune response. Both factors are beneficial for your fight against high-functioning anxiety.

You can easily create a balance in your emotions and start taking charge by spending a few hours daily or weekly in an activity that helps you to clarify and rest your mind. Meditation, yoga, tai chi, learning to decompress by listening to light music that makes you relax and feel good, will work by heightening your brain's left side responses, and thus increasing feelings of positivity. And that is the perfect start for letting go of all those negative emotions and thoughts that are weighing you down.

Learning to Accept What You Can't Change

Your next step in healing your high-functioning anxiety is to learn to accept what is. Strive to maintain a balance in your daily life and understand that not everything is within your control. No matter how hard you try, there are times when events and situations will work against you. If you learn to let those kinds of situations go, it will be freeing. Otherwise, you are going to add the burden of what you cannot control to the rest of the anxieties you already harbor.

Avoid obsessing over problems you are unable to control. Things that happen at the office, in school, or even at home can sometimes be beyond your control. Such situations are going to upset you; they will make you sad, angry, stressed, and anxious. In those times, do not try to hide your feelings.

Instead, try to understand them, along with why you are feeling those emotions. Only then you will realize that those emotions are baseless because the event or situation causing them is not within your control. Therefore, you must not react to them.

For example, your best friend invites you over to her house for dinner with other friends, but you have an important interview early the next morning. You want to get an early start and be fresh and alert for the interview, so you decline the invitation with an apology and an explanation.

Your friend gets upset and accuses you of making up excuses to avoid visiting her, going so far as to call you a bad friend. When that happens, your anxiety flares up and you feel terrible; you feel angry and hopeless.

But when you write down those emotions and why you are feeling them, you realize that your friend's unrealistic response to your genuine excuse was what caused them.

The interview is important to you, and so is your friend. But while you can visit her at another time and make future dinner plans, the interview is non-negotiable and deserves priority. At that moment, you realize your friend was being unrealistic and you have no control over her emotions or thoughts. And so, let go of stressing over events that are beyond your control and focus instead on the positive—that important interview you are looking forward to nailing with success!

Focus on What's Good for You

From the example above, did you realize that by acknowledging, and not ignoring your emotions and thoughts, you were able to clarify them and put your feelings into perspective?

That is how you learn to deflect the emotional suppression pattern of high-functioning anxiety and focus on the positive. At this point, I suggest you start updating the journal you started, to keep track of your worries and stress. Write down the negativities that you think are weighing you down.

Identify negative factors in your life and try to let go of them. Negative factors that make you feel worthless and unloved could even involve a toxic parent or friend. It could be a job you are unhappy in, a high standard of schoolwork you have set for yourself that is weighing you down, and so on. Try to identify such negativities; compile them into a list and see how you can fix them. In the case of a parent or friend, you can try talking to them and explaining how their interactions with you make you feel anxious and experience self-doubt.

If talking does not work, try to distance yourself from the toxic people in your life. Spend more time doing the things you like with the people who appreciate you for who you are, and always bring out the best in you.

Create a balance in your life by letting go of negativity and embracing positivity. It won't be easy, as your anxiety is going to keep trickling through every time you try to be positive, but as you practice your meditation and keep making conscious efforts to let go of what you cannot control, it is going to get easier.

Facing Your Fears

Make a list of what scares you, and from there, start planning to face those fears one at a time. Do not force yourself to overcome your fears all at once; start with the easy ones. If you dislike public gatherings and avoid any kind of social events, try to address that anxious fear by starting to attend small events. Go to a party at a friend's house or join a local club or group that's in line with your hobby and attend the weekly meetings. At office meetings, join in the conversations, instead of sitting quietly in the corner as you may normally do. In the same manner, try to address your fears by exposing yourself to them. Once you master your fear, you have built resilience against them, and they no longer have the power to harm you or cause anxiety.

Resilience Is a Stress Buster

Working on developing resilience is a powerful tool for busting your stress and controlling your anxiety-influenced emotions. It is a healthy option for developing a thicker skin against anxiety and giving in to all those doubts and fears.

Make sure your journal is well maintained, as it will be your tool for evaluating your day's experiences, putting your emotions, thoughts, and behavior into perspective. It will be your scale for balancing the negatives and positives in your life. Use your journal to jot down everything you feel, and then dissect it until you get to the root of that emotion, thought, or behavior, to understand why they took place and how to let go of the negativity. In the end, you must become immune to anxiety.

Improve Your Resilience with Do-It-Yourself Mental Health Checks

As you start putting the above techniques into practice, it is important to keep track of where you stand in terms of your mental health. Keeping a check on your mind from the start—when your anxiety issues began to manifest—would have helped you to address them before you even came to this stage. However, it is never too late to start, and doing regular assessments of your mental state will help you to keep your emotions and thoughts in check.

Getting Attuned to Your Feeling—How to Do the Scan

Start by checking your body, because the health of your mind is shown in your body. Make note of the following:

- Is your heart rate slow or elevated?
- Are your shoulders relaxed or tense?
- Is your chest light or do you feel tightness?

The latter symptoms suggest some form of anxiety. Pay more attention to your body and if you are dealing with anxiety, you will observe some tell-tale signs. These signs can include you habitually play with your hair, your foot taps almost involuntarily, and you constantly have sweaty palms. Watch out for a reoccurrence of your other symptoms such as avoidance behavior, becoming withdrawn or irritable, etcetera. Once you identify your typical symptoms, think of them as triggers you need to stop before they progress further. Doing so will help you to develop a self-help mechanism, such as deep-breathing and counting to ten, to deflect the anxiety that is building up inside you.

If your self-check reveals you are dealing with anxiety, then practice the methods we discussed in this chapter. Yoga, listening to calm music, deep breathing, meditation, are just a few great examples.

As well do a check of your emotions, determining what you are feeling at the time. Once you do, indulge in the exercises discussed by focusing on the positive and dispelling the negative.

Use Check-Ins to Decompress and Self-Reflect

Check-ins should be done daily, as that way you avoid

waiting for your anxiety levels to rise before you think of evaluating your mental situation. Have a daily set time, such as bedtime, for your daily check-in. The end of the day just before you settle down to sleep is ideal to reflect on your day; to think about the trials you went through, and the issues you had with people, events, and situations. Analyzing such events and coming to terms with your feelings will help you to understand and make sense of your emotions and even change the way you feel about some of them. Decompressing and self-reflecting will free your mind and help you to enjoy a restful night, which means you wake up with a fresh new resolve to tackle life's problems with plenty of resilience.

Ask yourself the following questions every time you practice self-reflection:

- How do I feel today?

Use this question to gauge your mood and to question why it is so. This is ideal for identifying your triggers and avoiding them in the future.

- What do I want to change?

Start by identifying changes that will help your anxiety. Identify how easy it is for you to put them into effect. As well, try making yourself willing to go the extra distance to do so.

- What are my needs?

Address your vulnerabilities. Do you expect more love, support, or understanding from family and friends? Do you need a change of environment? Analyze and identify your needs for a positive improvement.

- Am I praising myself?

Acknowledge your accomplishments; do not chalk them up to just another thing you do. Acknowledge that you achieved something good and give yourself the praise you deserve. Bump up your self-confidence and stop being pessimistic.

- What do I no longer need?

Let go of things or people you identify with as bringing you down. This could be a job that is zapping your energy, a need to work less in general, or a need to let go of always trying to be the best student in the class. Once you identify what you need to let go of, it may be difficult to make the changes immediately, but you can set things in motion to eventually get there.

Develop a Better Understanding of Yourself and the Cause and Effect of Your Emotions

Getting in tune with your feelings will help you to gauge where your emotions stem from. For example, if you feel overly sad over minor incidents such as a close colleague leaving the workplace, you can check in on that emotion without letting it get out of hand, as you are aware you are generally more emotional than others. Or if a friend is constantly making you feel worthless, you know you will end up feeling sad, angry, or in despair as you doubt yourself. Once you identify and realize the cause of those emotions is linked to the time spent with that friend, you can practice distancing yourself by avoiding interactions with them.

HOW DOES YOUR PERSONALITY INFLUENCE YOUR ANXIETY

A person's personality traits can be used to categorize them into Type-A and Type-B personalities.

I already mentioned that Type-A personalities were more vulnerable to anxiety-related syndromes because of, well, their personality. Based on a person's personality, a lot more than their anxiety levels can be determined. It is also possible to predict their physical health since their mind and body are interconnected.

Type-A Personality

People possessing this personality are more prone to stress because they are more intense. They are go-getters working on an agenda. They are also very competitive and always chasing goals. Their accomplishments, as well as the amount of effort they put into achieving their desires, are constantly under analysis by themselves, which makes them highly self-critical too.

Physical and Mental Traits

- Time rules their life.
- They are very proactive and always in a hurry; they walk, eat, and move fast.
- As they are highly ambitious, they feel they must always be doing something productive, and feel guilty when relaxing.
- They have a knack for handling several tasks at once. If you are Type-A, you are probably a great multi-tasker.

- Schedules rule their life and stopping to have fun is not on the schedule.
- They are go-getters; they want to be the best and aim high.
- Failure is not an option, and they will beat themselves up for any.
- They have nervous gestures that give away their instability hidden within. Tapping their fingers in impatience, clenching their fists, and even banging on surfaces with their hands when agitated are tell-tale signs.

Type-B Personality

This personality is almost on the opposite spectrum of Type-A personalities. Type Bs are laid back, more reflective of their lifestyle, and possess high levels of tolerance. As you can see, people with this type of personality will obviously have fewer stressors and live relatively simpler lives than Type-A personalities.

Physical and Mental Traits

- Time is not the ruler of their lives.
- They possess mild mannerisms.
- If they compete, it is to have fun and not necessarily to win.
- Deadlines—what deadlines? They are laid back and take life easy.
- The quality of life is what's important.
- Their lives are mostly stress free.

Which personality do you identify with more? Most people dealing with high-functioning anxiety possess Type-A characteristics. However, there is no rule to say that you must be Type-A if you have anxiety. Sometimes our personalities can be influenced by life events. A traumatic incident you faced, PTSD, prolonged illness, financial stress, an unhappy family life, or parents who do not appreciate your Type-B personality. These can influence and cause a change wherein, although you are Type-B, your circumstances have caused you to develop anxiety, whereby you start to display the traits of a Type-A personality.

Maybe you do so to prove a point, to please someone else, to avoid unpleasant outside influences; but it is possible that you could be hiding a Type-B personality under all that anxiety.

Even if you are a Type-A, if you look at the above traits, they can all be altered and toned down by practicing mindfulness and creating a balance between your emotions, thoughts, and behavior.

Bottom line: Nothing is impossible, you can achieve anything you set your mind to. Choosing your well-being by deciding to relax more, stress less, and choose laughter over clinging to unrealistic, sad emotions will triumph in the end.

In the next chapter, let's see if we can redeem some dignity for anxiety—can it really be a good trait? After all, anxiety is our automatic response to dealing with a traumatic event and as such, it may just keep us safe. Let's find out.

3

CAN ANXIETY BE GOOD?

"No need to hurry. No need to sparkle. No need to be anybody but oneself." —Virginia Woolf

A nxiety is a trait we have inherited to help us cope with traumatic events and to keep us safe. Sadly, anxiety, which helped keep our hunter-gatherer ancestors alert, fearful of danger, and ultimately alive, seems to be the bane of modern society because so many of us are being diagnosed with anxiety-related issues that are causing more damage than good.

In this chapter, let's look at anxiety in a kinder light and see how you can use your condition to your benefit. I will also help you to identify your triggers so you will know what to avoid and what not to do.

We will discuss choosing career paths to match your skills and strengths, as well as to help with your condition. Let's explore ways to manage your anxiety in the workplace and perhaps make the decision to change your career path and choose one that is healthier for you mentally and physically.

A LOOK AT THE EVOLUTIONARY SCIENCE OF ANXIETY

Before we get started, let's establish a very important fact: Humans live in what is called a "delayed return environment." This means that our actions are sometimes aimed at rewards we will get in the future. These rewards include working long hours in the office, months on end, to afford a holiday abroad in summer—your delayed reward.

On the flip side, a living being who lives in an immediate return environment will have very basic needs. A fine example is animals, as they have very few needs, and therefore every action they take is for an immediate reward.

When your pet dog is hungry, he will point to his food bowl which you refill, and thus his action of pointing got him his immediate reward—food. People are much more complex and need to feel their future is secure and will therefore labor a lot more to make sure their delayed return environment is taken care of.

Despite all our modern needs for future security, human beings started to shift into the delayed return environment just under 500 years ago.

Before that, we were just simple beings with simple immediate return needs. While our brains remain about the same as they were in the Paleolithic era, over 200 thousand years ago, our modern needs have had an accelerated increase in just the past 100 years.

Nearly everything that modern humans know and identify with has only existed for close to a century. This includes cars, television, planes, branded clothes, computers, smartphones, and the internet.

Since the evolution of early humans, which happened over seven million years ago, your brain has been evolving and getting accustomed to a simple immediate return environment.

While your brain's evolution took millions of years, the delayed return environment took only a hundred years to fast-track into the modern era. And this new development was way too fast for our slow-developing brains to keep up. Think about it: We are still running on the same brain prototype as our ancient Paleolithic ancestors. As a result, our brains *must* still be struggling to adjust and keep up.

Teaching Old Brains New Tricks—Formula for Trouble

Chronic stress in modern humans can be blamed on the fact that we are using an old brain prototype to try and keep up with the environmental changes of delayed returns.

In the past, before human needs evolved and complicated things, stress, worry, and anxiety were the good guys; they worked as a team to keep our ancestors safe and alive.

- In the past: The thought of running low on food as winter approached, would start to worry you. You would stress over not finding food and starving during the harsh snow falls ahead, and so your anxiety makes you take action. You go hunting, gather some berries and nuts to store in your cave, and operate with caution during the cold winter months. Problem solved; your stress and anxiety disappear as your immediate return environment needs are met.
- In modern times: You worry about the cost of turning on the heaters during winter. You are also dreaming of a winter break in the tropics, but you know that a big promotion is coming up and you don't want to take time off from work. You worry about the doctor's warning that you are pre-diabetic and so you try to bring down your blood sugar by cutting out sweets and suddenly life is very boring.

All these are plans for a delayed return environment, which is quite stressful, leaving you wishing life was simpler.

Living in our delayed return environment is tough. We are stuck in this endless cycle of setting up our future, but unfortunately for most of us, that rosy and secure future never comes because we are burned out long before it.

Trying to meet the demands of a delayed return environment is one of the greatest reasons for so many people being diagnosed with anxiety disorders.

How Can You Avoid the Stress of a Delayed Return Environment

The biggest challenge in managing a delayed return environment is working hard for an uncertain future. Although you work hard for a promotion, there is no guarantee you will receive it. No matter how much effort and care you put into raising your children, or providing them with a good education, there is no guarantee they are going to end up successful in life. We end up suffering from a range of anxiety disorders that crop up because we are trying to fit into an environment that was not designed for our well-being.

Listed below are some tried and tested methods to make that uncertainty more plausible and less stressful.

1. Change Your Outlook and Look for Short-Term Rewards

It is easy to shift your focus from a stressful future event and find satisfaction in short-term solutions, thereby reaping the rewards of an immediate return environment in which your brain is more adaptable. To do this, you need to shift your focus or your anxiety to a more short-term worry.

As an example, your doctor advises you, that you are borderline diabetic. You stress over your rising blood sugar levels, as well as the future, where you'll have to deal with a chronic disease, thereby becoming another statistic. You can stress over this future result, and perhaps develop some type of anxiety disorder in time, or you can consider a short-term solution and concentrate on eating a healthier diet.

Planning your week's meals so you're not eating food that causes an immediate spike in your blood sugar levels is a good short-term solution. You will be rewarded with peace of mine and a sense of accomplishment once you meet those needs. The same theory works for your schoolwork; you study hard and ace those immediate exams and perhaps, worry about getting into an Ivy League school when the time comes. But for now, you work to meet the short-term worries and stresses which get resolved in an immediate return environment.

Those were just two examples; you can work on similar solutions to reduce the long-term anxiety you are battling and enjoy short-term solutions to your worries.

2. Quantify Your Actions

Quantifying your actions will not solve your anxiety problems, but it will reduce your worry. For example, you have decided you want to lose weight to maintain good health.

In this case, instead of looking at losing 22 pounds in the long-term and stressing endlessly—where you might end up binge eating because of the anxiety—you can quantify how often you plan to visit the gym to lose weight and get fit.

By focusing on the number of visits to the gym, you are deflecting your mind from the worry of losing weight. And by simply concentrating on meeting those weekly gym visits, you have not only reduced your long-term weight loss anxiety—you have most likely started losing weight as well.

Quantifying what you must accomplish will always deflect the stress of long-term goals. It may not cure your anxiety or stress, but it will help you to focus on factors that offer you a chance to enjoy an immediate return environment.

The Evolutionary Link to Your Fight or Flight Response to Anxiety

You are most likely familiar with the fight or flight response when you have a panic attack and anxiety takes over. The threat posed by an event or situation will get your pulse racing, your pupils will dilate, breathing may become labored, and you'll break into a sweat. These are symptoms that in the past alerted our hunter-gatherer ancestors of impending dangers, so they could decide on an immediate course of action.

However, in modern society, the fight or flight response is triggered by a variety of factors, including when you are in danger or feel threatened. When you have high-functioning anxiety or any other mental health condition, your fight or flight response is increased, and you are more sensitive to triggers than if you do not have anxiety disorders.

The Fight or Flight Response—Hyperarousal

Acute stress response—which is your fight or flight response —is triggered by your brain, which becomes alert to threats or dangers sending signals throughout your nervous system. The result is several physical symptoms taking place at once.

When these physical changes happen, your body starts to secrete hormones, noradrenaline, and adrenaline. These hormones get you ready to fight or to make a hasty retreat.

- Your breathing increases and your heart starts to beat rapidly, in turn increasing your pulse rate and supply of oxygen, altogether helping you to take swift action or sustain a fight.
- Your muscles tense and glycogen stored in them gets converted into energy, which makes you stronger to fight or flee the situation.
- You start to clench your fists.
- Your pupils become dilated, letting in more light, thus improving your night vision.

These actions induce an automatic response from you, which is why you spring into action, sometimes before having time to process what's happening. For example, you jump out of the way of a moving vehicle that suddenly veers too close to the curb. Or a sudden stop of a vehicle in front of you causes you to slam on the brakes.

While these responses were designed to keep you safe, a mental disorder can trigger the emotion in an unnatural, uncomfortable, and inconvenient manner.

When brought on by acute stress, the fight or flight response can be controlled by being conscious of what's happening to you. While you cannot control when and where the reflex takes place, you can make note of the triggers and try to avoid them by practicing techniques to calm down.

How to Calm You Fight or Flight Response

The following techniques will help you to calm down and get your panic attacks under control. Through constant practice, you will get better at it, and start the calming techniques the moment you notice a trigger that sets off your fight or flight response.

1. Deep Breaths to Slow Your Breathing, Your Heart Rate, and Your Adrenaline Percentage

Learn to calm down with deep breathing. As your heart begins to race and your breathing becomes labored, you trigger the production of adrenaline, which will shoot up your energy levels and heart rate. This is a very uncomfortable phenomenon to deal with when you are struggling with anxiety issues. Deep breathing will help your heartbeat to slow down, and as you start to relax, your muscles lose their tension, with your adrenaline levels dropping as well.

Taking up yoga is a good practice for learning more about deep breathing techniques, which you can apply to deal with anxiety attacks. You may not be able to practice a proper yogi stance of breathing while in public, but where possible, move away from the crowds and find a quiet corner to practice your deep breathing until your fight or flight response has calmed down.

2. Calming Techniques

Imagery is a good technique to help you calm down when faced with an uncomfortable situation that is causing your anxiety to build up. Visualize yourself away from the situation and in a calmer, happier place. Any place that brings you happiness will do the trick.

Chanting or repeating an empowering phrase while you practice deep breathing is another helpful method. Close your eyes and repeat something that works for you. For example, *"I am calm, I have nothing to worry about, and this feeling is going to pass."* You can choose any phrase that will help you to calm down; once selected, keep repeating it until your anxiety attack passes.

Next, let's look at some common triggers and how you can identify and avoid them to curtail your anxiety attacks.

RECOGNIZING YOUR ANXIETY TRIGGERS

It is important to identify anxiety triggers to develop better coping mechanisms and avoid placing yourself in situations that trigger your anxiety.

An anxiety trigger is a very specific event, place, action, or even a reason that acts as a trigger to get your anxiety going.

Anxiety attacks can be caused by external environmental factors or internal triggers such as an illness. Asthma, for example, can lead to a panic attack if you are faced with an asthma attack without your inhaler. This type of panic reaction can be deadlier than the disease itself and lead to serious fatalities. The severity of a panic attack can be fatal, regardless of the disease.

Sometimes triggers work beyond causing anxiety, as they can lead to panic attacks which at times can be very severe and hard to deal with. The symptoms we discussed earlier in the fight or flight response are a form of heightened anxiety that can become very hard to bear.

Common Anxiety Triggers

- Health complications, heart issues, asthma, low blood sugar, and hyperthyroidism.
- Medicines prescribed for common health problems, such as the flu, or birth control trigger a hormonal reactions and other complications leading to an anxiety attack.
- Caffeine is a trigger and will worsen your symptoms.
- Stress that occurs due to exterior events, failing an exam, losing a promotion, finances.
- A conflict with your loved one, your spouse, your parents, or your children.

- Social anxiety triggers including fear of being in a crowd, public speaking, making small talk at parties, or anything that takes you out of your comfort zone.
- Poor sleep which builds up fatigue.
- A shift in your normal lifestyle. These can include having your first baby, starting a new school, or joining a new office. Things that alter your normal routine and change the environment you are comfortable in.

You may be dealing with different triggers, as well as some I have mentioned. Therefore, it is important to identify your personal triggers.

To do so, you can adapt the following techniques:

- Pull out your handy journal once more. Mark a section for your triggers. Every time you endure a panic attack or heightened anxiety that was brought on suddenly, write down the events leading up to the situation and backtrack. This way you'll be able to identify exactly who, what, or when your anxiety was triggered. You may find a way to avoid such triggers in the future, or you can prepare yourself to calm down the next time you become exposed to those triggers.
- Think back to any type of trauma you may have endured as a child or as an adult. Maybe you witnessed a serious car accident and therefore, every time you see a car speeding on the street, your anxiety is triggered. Try to delve into your past and see if you can make a connection.
- Avoid internal triggers. Apart from caffeine, there might be other food types that trigger your anxiety by increasing your adrenaline or heart rate. Analyze your past attacks and try to define if this is the case for you.

- Talk to a friend or loved one. Sometimes the people you are close to will have more insight into your behavior than you do. Your spouse or close friend, for example, may have observed situations that make you panic. They may know the triggers that lead to you becoming agitated and anxious. A good talk with people who are close to you can reveal a lot about your nature which you may not be aware of yourself. This is especially true if you are dealing with high-flying anxiety, and you have blocked your mind from influences other than those perceived by your anxiety-fueled mind.

I did promise you that we would look at the benefits of anxiety, so let's get to that fascinating subject next.

How Can I Use Anxiety to My Benefit

Dealing with your anxiety issues daily can be frustrating and downright exhausting. Your social life is affected, you are uptight and moody most of the time, and you dread triggers that will cause the next panic attack. But what if I told you that just like in prehistoric times, anxiety could be used to your advantage?

It can be done, as I have listed in the points below:

- Anxiety can keep you safe.

Anxiety is your response to fear, and we discussed how anxiety-induced changes within you, both physically and mentally, allow you to react to a dangerous situation. There are times when anxiety can be painful, such as, when it makes you feel like no one wants to spend time with you. While such notions will add to your stress, worry, and feelings of sadness or isolation, they will also help you to become guarded about who can hurt your feelings. Therefore, use anxiety as a forewarning in such instances, but make sure you identify the real emotion from the fake to stop yourself from overreacting to situations.

- You are more critical and become smarter due to anxiety.

People with anxiety overanalyze everything. They look deeper into a cause, event, or situation, to determine if it is safe, necessary, and practical. Consequently, you become smarter and more critical as you learn. Keeping in mind your quest for better understanding anxiety will allow you to explore it more, and that research will lead you down so many different paths that will help make you more aware of how the human mind and society works.

- Anxiety keeps drawing your attention to important tasks.

By paying more attention to the reasons behind your anxiety triggers, you become more attuned to your specific needs, fears, and strengths. Anxiety helps you to discover more intimate details about your personality.

- You become an overachiever

While this trait cannot be sustained in the long run, due to the heavy toll on your mind and body, anxiety *does* help you to become an overachiever. Fueled by anxiety, you push yourself beyond limits to be a perfectionist, which is a common trait of high-functioning anxiety, and you will therefore be able to reach your full potential. The downside is that you burn out when you become an anxiety-fueled overachiever. By setting limits to everything you do, you can continue to reap these benefits and avoid burnout.

- Channel your energy fueled by anxiety to make yourself better.

While some people will become overachievers, others suffering from anxiety and depression will become totally immobile. Getting out of bed is an effort on most days. Still, your anxiety levels keep building, while fears, frustrations, and stresses are all coiled up and ready to spring. That is what I call your "bottled-up energy." Go ahead and use that energy by channeling it into your tasks.

Did you ever stay home all-day watching movies instead of going out? Then, suddenly, you get hyperactive and decide you are going to clean the house and perhaps go for a walk. That is that pent-up energy you harnessed because the anxiety within you was making you restless. Go ahead and use your pent-up energy to fuel your day's chores and you will have conquered anxiety, at least for a day.

The above points have been listed for you to see the silver lining in anxiety. But by no means are they foolproof plans, and I realize they can be downright damaging when you are dealing with high-functioning anxiety. However, if you can channel the good aspect of anxiety through each point, I encourage you to try the reasoning and see where you can find benefits.

CHOOSING A CAREER TO SUIT YOUR NEEDS

Avoiding anxiety triggers is important, and a major trigger for most people is their job. The career they have chosen is the wrong one. Therefore, they suffer not only anxiety, but the risk of dealing with occasional panic attacks at the workplace.

Staying in a career that is feeding your anxiety is also not going to help you heal.

There are plenty of rewarding and fulfilling jobs you can explore, even with high levels of anxiety—what's important is finding the right fit.

Explore Your Mind, Scour Your Needs

There are no specific jobs that are designed for people with anxiety disorders. However, there are career choices and jobs that help you realize your full potential, develop your hidden talents, and bring total satisfaction to your life. Identifying your skills, strengths, dreams, and goals is the first step in finding that type of career.

The anxiety workbook journal I have offered in addition to this book can be a great tool for achieving this type of clarity. Chapter 7 will show you how to use a journal, and how to separate your emotions and thoughts to arrive at conclusions and decisions. Follow the steps with the aid of the workbook journal and you can easily put your skills, strengths, and more into perspective.

- List everything you have a talent for. Are you an artist? Maybe you can follow a career as an illustrator. Are you skilled with numbers, or is cooking your passion? List your abilities in your journal workbook for evaluation and arriving at the decisions.
- List your skills, what you are passionate about, and your strengths. Combining your educational background with your skills will help you narrow down the types of work that you will enjoy. Having an education in economics and a skill for picking up great bargains may make you a good salesperson or a shop manager.

- Identify any additional qualifications you may need to obtain your dream job. If you want to be a florist, maybe you need to learn more about horticulture and creating floral displays.
- Write down all the jobs you liked in the past, and what you liked about them. This will help you to narrow down what you will enjoy in a career choice.
- List your stresses. Be realistic; you may be a high-flier working in the stock market, but if that job is triggering your anxiety levels too often, it could be a sign that a change in careers and a healthier option is what you need. In addition, it's time to consider a job in terms of longevity, because as you know, living with high levels of stress is a sure-fire way to cut your life short.
- On the flip side, just because a job is challenging, there is no need to shun it. People who are dealing with high-functioning anxiety are very adept at meeting challenges, sticking to deadlines, and extremely organized. You may be no different, so don't let job challenges scare you off; you probably possess lots of untapped potential and strengths within.

Some Job Options That May Work for You

Below are some options I have found which may work well for people dealing with anxiety issues. You may not find what you like in the list, but that should not stop you from exploring your possibilities.

Mental Health Worker or a School Guidance Counselor

Who better to offer help and understanding to other people suffering from a mental health condition than you? You won't just be diagnosing people based on theories in books, instead, you will be putting your heart and soul into your work, showing empathy, and understanding from a very personal level. If you feel this is the right job for you, check out your options, along with which qualifications you are required to obtain to function as a guidance counselor or a mental health worker.

Landscape Artist

Put your knack for attention to detail to good use by trying out a job as a florist or a landscape artist, or perhaps even a talented gardener. Not only will you be harnessing your creative talents for these jobs, but you will be working relatively alone with nature, which is one of the most calming factors for anxiety-driven minds.

Technician or Analyst

Any type of analytical job will fit you and your compulsion to analyze details. Lab technicians work through a collection of samples and analyses. Medical lab technicians use blood samples, to help diagnose ailments or medical conditions in patients. While an Environmental lab technician or a Marine lab technician will analyze the environment and oceans to try and find solutions to pollution and the disruption of marine life. Again, these are jobs where you work on your own, using your analytical and deduction skills.

Tradesperson

Working as a tradesperson, specializing in a particular trade, will focus your energy on the job at hand. An electrician, carpenter, or plumber requires hands-on work, and you certainly have no time to spend thinking about your anxiety. These types of physical jobs are very good for getting your mind off the stresses and worries of your high-functioning anxiety.

Computer Technician / Software Developer

This job requires plenty of focus on things like troubleshooting, repairing, installing, and maintaining hardware and software, and other issues that crop up when using computers. The role of a software developer is particularly interesting because one can harness their strengths and fears to create software that fills a need based on their experiences and their knowledge.

Be a Freelancer

Work at your own pace and at your own times when you choose to work freelance. There is no dealing with teams or bosses when you work freelance because you are your own boss, and the amount of energy and effort you throw into your work will reflect how successful you can become.

House Painter

Here is another peaceful and calming job you can enjoy while managing your anxiety. A painter is often someone who is very creative and manages to brighten up even the dullest of spaces. Enjoy job satisfaction and letting out your creative spirit.

Other jobs that fit into the categories I have mentioned include land surveyors, pet care professionals, librarian advocates, accountants, vehicle mechanics, and radiology technicians.

There is a whole range of exciting options out there for you to choose from. Never hold back, but try instead to work around your anxiety, and you will find your niche.

Next, we move on to healing your mind with a more in-depth view of the techniques we have already discussed. Meditation is a valuable practice for anyone to use when they need to recalibrate their mind, body, and soul. You learned about mindful meditation, so now let's look at more facts to help you understand the benefits of meditation for healing the mind.

4

_____

HEAL YOUR MIND

"So much time and effort is spent on wanting to change, trying to change, to be somebody different, better, or new. Why not use this time to get comfortable with yourself as you are, instead?"
—Andy Puddicombe, Headspace co-founder

Your mind is a delicate accessory you possess and taking care of it—nurturing and strengthening your emotions and thoughts—is an important factor that makes up one point of the anxiety triangle.

In this chapter, we will look at the power of meditation to soothe your mind; to help you to rejuvenate your mind, body, and soul to free your spirit so that your thoughts lose their turmoil, and your mind has time to breathe and relax.

Meditation sharpens your mental awareness and helps you become more sensitive to your triggers, thereby helping you to calm down before you endure heightened anxiety or a panic attack.

Meditation helps you to focus on what is important. Remember, we are struggling with the challenges of coping with our delayed return environment, and therefore we forget to live in the moment, absorb the present, and feel and enjoy those simple moments when our lives are truly balanced and blessed. On the contrary, our minds are typically wandering, as we try to figure out how we are going to balance our day's schedule with so many things we want to—and have—to do.

We wonder about obtaining the best grades in school, about making more money, and thus aiming for a promotion, although it means longer hours at the office and less time at home with family. These are all cliches that have been analyzed and researched, yet nothing has changed with our habits; in fact, the statistics prove that anxiety disorders are increasing among the US population.

Between 2006 and 2018, anxiety among the US adult population increased from 5.12% to 6.68%, with an alarming increase of 7.97% to 14.66% among young adults in the 18–25 age group (Goodwin et al., 2020).

While we cannot fight the statistics or the increasing anxiety triggers and lifestyles that encourage them, we can strive to take care of ourselves. Our mental and physical beings will serve us well when we are kinder to their needs. Therefore, in this chapter, we will start with nourishing and healing your mind.

THE BENEFITS OF MEDITATION

The use of meditation to calm and reduce your anxieties, as well as to improve your anterior brain activity—triggering your feel-good emotions—has already been discussed. Next, let's examine the overall benefits of meditation to help you develop a more positive outlook in life, improve your concentration, and sleep better. All of these are factors that will help with controlling the challenges you face with high-functioning anxiety.

1. Learn to Feel Good About Yourself

Improve your self-worth to have a positive outlook in life. Mindful meditation is one of the best tools mental health researchers use for managing anxiety, stress, and depression.

Studies were conducted on the benefits of meditation for controlling negativity; people who were enrolled in a meditation program recorded improved control over negative thoughts as opposed to the group of people who did no meditation therapies (Kiken & Shook, 2014).

Another study confirmed that levels of inflammation cytokines were reduced with meditation. Cytokines are a protein substance; inflammation cytokines are released when your body sends out stress signals from a trauma, such as an injury. The response is inflammation, which helps the injured area to heal. However, sometimes inflammation can occur or continue when it is not necessary.

Sometimes, long after the injured cells in a traumatized area of your body have healed, the inflammation continues, leading to many degenerative diseases such as cancers, in turn causing the cells to mutate and become corrupt. That prolonged state of inflammation that is damaging to your body is called "chronic inflammation."

Anxiety and depression stimulate the release of cortisol, which in turn influences the secretion of cytokines. However, studies have confirmed that meditation is a multifaceted practice that influences cognition and the secretion of hormones, as well as improves sensory skills. In addition, the nervous system helps to reduce the number of cytokines in the bloodstream (Kasala et al., 2014).

2. Mental and Physical Stress Buster to Help You Sleep Better

Meditation is a very good stress buster that helps soothe both your mental and physical state. The release of cortisol due to stress and depression leads to a range of problems such as insomnia, lowered alertness, high blood pressure, and feeling unnaturally tired. Mindful meditation has shown an improvement in the above conditions, as well as some physical ailments such as irritable bowel syndrome (IBS).

Improved sleep quality is one of the best benefits, meditation offers to people dealing with the challenges of high-functioning anxiety and its daily trials.

3. Promotes Emotional Self-Regulation

This happens when you become more self-aware of your strengths through meditation. Self-regulation is the ability to understand and consciously control your behavior, emotions, and thoughts. The calming effects of meditation, which encourages self-awareness, helps you to come to terms with yourself; you develop an understanding of your strengths and weaknesses, in turn allowing you to control how badly anxiety affects you.

Meditation offers people dealing with anxiety-related issues a chance to build on their self-efficiency; a trait that helps you to overcome problems such as pessimism, which often plagues the mind of someone with high-functioning anxiety. It is caused by low self-esteem and the perception that they have no friends and won't fit in with society.

The improved mental and physical changes promoting self-regulation and self-awareness are attributed to improvements in your social life, as well as the enjoyment of other people's company, which occurs naturally once you become more self-aware of your own positive traits and strengths. Meditation is the best path to get there because it stills your anxious and negative thoughts long enough for the positive side of your emotions and thoughts to filter through.

Remember that meditation is a tool you carry with you wherever you go; all you need is a quiet spot. Mindful meditation can be practiced anywhere while doing anything once you master the technique. Until then, practice breathing and walking meditations as I explained in Chapter 2.

Types of Meditation for Anxiety

There is no need to enroll in a class if you don't have the time or the money to do so. Meditation can be practiced within the comfort of your own home, dorm room, or any quiet location. A quiet spot outdoors, such as under the shade of a tree in the park or at the beach will do.

To meditate, you are not required to sit cross-legged and chant 'om' like a seasoned yogi—that belongs in the movies. Instead, to meditate and guide your thoughts, you can indulge in any one of the following exercises.

Make sure to keep up consistency and get in at least a 30-minute session per day. While at first it may seem tough to stop your negative thoughts from filtering through, in time you will learn to override them. Meditation is not wholly about stopping your flow of thoughts, rather it is a time for you to recalibrate, to put into perception your challenges, and to understand yourself from an exterior point of view—because through meditation, you get to look at yourself from the outside.

1. Mindfulness Meditation

This type of meditation is straightforward and is no more complicated than its name suggests. Therefore, mindful meditation implies being mindful of exactly what you are doing at that exact moment. This could be walking in the park, washing the car, or taking your dog for a walk. There can be no in-between little thoughts entering your mind.

You know how many little thoughts dot your mind whenever you are engaged in an activity. You could be sitting in an important meeting, but your mind could be sorting through several different issues, including where your next vacation is going to be.

Mindfulness meditation means you concentrate on just the task at hand. If you are vacuuming the floor, you concentrate on just that—100%. No vacuuming while planning out dinner or thinking about what you need to buy from the grocery store. You must think about vacuuming and nothing else.

Although mindfulness meditation sounds easy when explained this way, it is not easy to master at once, and therefore it requires plenty of practice. To start with, practice a more grounded type of meditation.

2. Breath Meditation

Initiate yourself into mindfulness meditation by focusing on your breathing; practicing your breathing meditation in a quiet corner is easy.

Here's the part where you get to sit cross-legged like in the movies, but still without the chanting. Sit down and practice inhaling and exhaling for five minutes. In those five minutes, concentrate on inhaling; feel the air fill your lungs and hold it before you exhale. Be conscious of the rise of your chest; how it expands with the air, and then exhale. As you do so, feel the air pass through your nostrils and be very conscious about the fall of your chest. Pause a moment and then repeat inhaling.

This method is meant to teach yourself to focus and be aware of what you are doing at that exact moment. It will still your thoughts, as well as those anxieties tearing you apart; these will become quiet, and you will feel a sense of relief and solidarity.

Once you master the technique of mindful breathing, you can move on to other tasks and start to practice mindfulness meditation.

Through this technique, you are teaching your brain to let go of its focus on stress and anxiety and focus instead on what you are doing in the moment. With this breathing exercise, you will reduce the amount of fight or flight responses generated by your amygdala.

This kind of regulation is not only ideal for reducing the amount of stress and anxiety your mind is dealing with daily, but in doing so, you are also lowering your markers for developing depression.

3. Walking Meditation

In this type of meditation, you use walking as a focus by concentrating on every footstep you take.

To do this, you must be 100% attuned to what you are doing: Lifting your foot off the ground, placing your heel first on the surface of the ground, then lifting the other foot and placing it in front of you in the same manner. You are walking consciously; something you would have been doing automatically since mastering your walking techniques as a toddler.

You create mind-body awareness this way, which will help you make a connection with your mental and physical being. It is ideal if you dislike sitting for long periods, as breathing meditation requires. Just ten minutes of mindful walking is enough to help you reduce your stress and anxiety levels.

As you indulge in the exercise, you will begin to realize that you can free your mind from the burdens of self-doubt, fear, worry, panic, and stress. Those constant feelings of doom will disappear in those ten minutes, as you teach your mind to be free and focus on thoughts away from your stresses.

4. The Loving and Kindness Meditation, or Mantra Meditation

This will teach you about self-worth and dispelling those terrible demeaning thoughts you have of yourself. Instead, you will learn to accept and love yourself for who you are. The exercise helps to encourage positive thoughts toward yourself to heal your pessimistic attitude, while encouraging you to become more tolerant of, and kinder towards others.

To practice loving and kindness meditation, find a comfortable spot to sit down. Then, focus on yourself. Do not let those thoughts of self-doubt enter your mind. "I am worthless," and "there is nothing I can do right," are the kind of thoughts you are going to try and flip around.

As you sit comfortably in a quiet, undisturbed spot, tell yourself "I am happy because I deserve to be happy" or "I am strong, and I can face my challenges."

Before you begin, write down a few phrases you want to emphasize in your meditation. Any self-worth-deflecting issues you feel should be addressed can be added to the list.

For example, you are constantly telling yourself you do not deserve to be in such a good relationship with a loving partner because you are not deserving of their love. Try and change your mind set by telling yourself you *are* deserving.

"I am deserving of a loving relationship because I too, am special."

Repeat the phrase over and over until you manage to convince yourself it is the truth. Alternatively, you can do this at least until you start to feel a shift in your mind, where you now focus on your real thoughts and not those influenced by your anxiety condition.

5. Tai Chi, the Gentle Flowing Movement of Chinese Martial Arts

A docile form of Chinese martial arts, tai chi helps you to calm and still your mind while indulging in a series of slow-paced movements and poses. The practice teaches grace and has a gentle demeanor that is calming, even to the onlooker.

6. Qigong and Ancient Remedy

Regarded as an ancient Chinese medication, qigong combines breathing, relaxation, meditation, and fluid movements to help your mind and body achieve a sense of relaxation and self-awareness. The practice is meant to have mental and physical curative powers that stem from reduced anxiety levels.

7. Yoga for Overall Well-Being

Through yoga, you obtain physical flexibility, you learn to calm yourself through breathing, and you're able to reach a calm plateau in your mind through meditation. The complex poses which require you to maintain balance and stabilized breathing require strong concentration. As such, it reduces the time your mind spends on your anxiety issues. Yoga is a wonderful distraction for the anxiety-riddled mind.

Tips to Build Healthy Meditation Habits

Make daily meditation an easy practice with these tips:

- Don't be overly ambitious. Start with miniature 30-minute sessions to ease your mind into the practice.
- Be flexible with time. Start by choosing a time you are less busy; perhaps a time when the rest of the family is still asleep. Or if you are not a morning person, try an evening session. Experiment with different times according to your schedule until you find the right fit. Do not try to make meditation a part of your busy schedule. Think of it as fine chocolate you keep, to savor at your leisure.
- Make yourself relax. Keep in mind that sitting cross-legged is good *only* if you are comfortable. Feel free to choose any pose that works for you, because being comfortable is the only criterion.
- Use apps or podcasts. There are plenty of YouTube videos and apps, as well as podcasts you can use to follow a meditation session. Again, experiment until you find what suits you.
- Do not expect immediate results. A wandering mind will indicate your awareness of what is happening and that is a start to developing a sharper, more controlled mind.

My Meditation Chart

Remember for meditation to work and for you to reap its full benefits, consistency is key. Therefore, I am including a chart like the one included in my workbook. it to set your goals and keep track of your daily progress. The chart also includes a space to add your thoughts, which will help you to gauge your emotional progress as your sessions increase.

Week: 1	My Meditation Goal (Tick each day you meditate)	Duration I Meditated (Increase time each day)	Where I Will Meditate (Decide where depending on your schedule)	My Thoughts (Record how you feel each day. Include improvements in your negative emotions and thoughts, as well as any self-awareness breakthrough you made while meditating)
Monday				
Tuesday				
Wednesday				
Thursday				
Friday				
Saturday				
Sunday				

Next, we move on to healing your physical being. Let's explore the many techniques available to help you achieve balance both mentally and physically.

5

PHYSICAL THERAPIES TO HEAL ANXIETY

"Yoga does not just change the way we see things; it transforms the person who sees." —B.K.S Iyengar

This chapter is about taking care of your physical being to improve your mental health. The benefits of yoga and massage therapy are well documented and encompass self-healing, rejuvenating the body, and enriching the mind.

THE PHYSICAL AND EMOTIONAL BENEFITS OF YOGA

Yoga focuses on your body's natural ability to self-heal. The main goal of yoga is to achieve harmony, strength, and awareness for overall physical and mental well-being.

You will achieve these benefits through simple stretching exercises, poses, breathing techniques, as well as flexing and stretching your muscles. To say yoga is a good fitness plan for anyone to adopt is not wrong, which is why many people, including people dealing with serious medical illnesses, choose to do it.

Yoga is a flexible practice, and like meditation, it offers several options to choose from, which means being a novice is not a problem. You can start slow and easy, until you are more comfortable with it. Your fitness levels have absolutely no bearing on the success of your yoga, and you certainly will not be expected to tie yourself up in knots or wrap your leg around your shoulder.

Benefits of Yoga

The physical benefits of yoga are numerous. Yoga is believed to lower blood pressure, lessen back pain, heal headaches, and even help with arthritis. Here is a list of benefits yoga has been known to offer to those who follow its methods.

Physical Benefits

- Improved sleep quality and reduction of insomnia symptoms.
- Better flexibility.
- More vitality, energy, and respiration.
- Weight reduction.
- Toning and strengthening muscles.
- Better blood circulation.
- Possible reduction of heart ailments.
- Possible improved stamina and athletic performance.

Mental Benefits

Helping with stress management is one of the biggest mental benefits that yoga has to offer. Remember how we learned about your emotional struggles manifesting themselves as physical ailments?

Therefore, neck pains, backaches, sleep disruptions, bad

headaches, and substance abuse can all be linked to stresses of the mind emerging as stresses of the body. Yoga can address most of these ailments and will work by improving your power of concentration, which will help you self-regulate and thus control your stresses.

Proper breathing techniques and poses will give you mental clarity and will, in turn, help you to manage anxiety triggers or patterns. Yoga can help you to relax your body and focus your mind on what is important, which is positivity and not the negativity that prevails because of your anxiety.

Easy First Step Yoga Postures and Their Benefits

Listed below are five popular poses you would learn as a newbie in a yoga class. Each pose offers a specific set of benefits, that stretch and tone your muscles, as well as help calibrate your mental status. At the end of this section is a set of instructions on how to follow each pose.

1. Tadasana

This pose is a vital posture you must master. A basic pose that is often a part of other yoga postures, tadasana is better known in English as the "mountain pose." This pose helps you find your center and create awareness, while promoting balance.

2. Bitilasana/Marjaryasana

This pose, known also as the "cat pose," takes care of your core and is good for addressing back and posture issues, especially if you are stuck at a desk job all day.

3. Virabhadrasana I

Also called the "warrior I pose," this pose is the first in a series. The posture is designed to loosen your chest and hips, as well as building strength in your legs while stretching and toning both leg and arm muscles. Holding this pose will help improve not only your balance, but your concentration as well.

4. Virabhadrasana II

This is a variation of the previous warrior pose. And while offering the same benefits where your quads are strengthened, the "warrior II" pose is good for flexing your hip muscles and is loved for improving flexibility.

5. Adho Mukha Svanasana

An excellent pose for stretching your back, hamstrings, arms, and shoulders, this pose— often called the "downward-facing dog"—is a good pose for finding your balance and calming your mind.

6. Balasana

Also called the "child's pose," this posture is one of the easiest to perform and is designed to help you reset and relax. While helping your nervous system calm down, the pose is also a good interlude you can use in class to enjoy a short rest in between the harder poses.

7. Shawavasa

The "corpse pose" may look unimportant after all those

complicated poses, but it is considered the most therapeutic. Here is the moment you spend in meditation relaxing in a state of calm, while also relieving stress, and helping your mind to be still.

HOW TO DO EASY FIRST STEP YOGA POSTURES

Tadasana

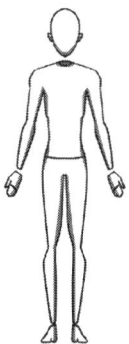

- Place your arms by your side with your palms facing forward, external rotation of arms.
- Stand with your feet hip distance apart.
- Press your feet to the ground, making sure to feel contact with the floor from all four corners of your foot.
- Your pelvis should be stacked over the feet, tighten your thigh muscles, and tuck in your tailbone.
- Lengthen your spine and inhale while simultaneously extending your arms up and above your head, then spread them out to the back of your head, with palms outstretched. Exhale and unclench your shoulder blades, moving them back and away from your head.

While doing so, slowly let your arms fall back down to your sides.

Marjaryasana / Bitilasana

- Start by placing your hands and knees on the floor, stack shoulders over your wrists, and hips over your knees.
- Tighten your abs and loosen your spine. Take a deep breath in.
- Slowly start to exhale, and as you do, arch your spine upward and bend your head down, tucking in your chin toward your chest, spreading your shoulder blades apart.
- Make sure your neck is loose.
- Inhale again, this time making a downward arch with your spine while relaxing your abs,
- Raise your head and keep your gaze slightly forward, do not push pressure on your neck.
- Push your pelvis forward and draw your shoulder blades together.

Virabhadrasana I

- Start by standing tall and straight (Tadasana) a mountain pose.
- Inhale, and then as you begin to exhale, move your left leg behind you by sliding your left foot about four feet back.
- Bend your right knee as you do this, so you look as though you are lunging. Front knee should be stacked over the front ankle.
- Press into your heel and big toe of the back foot.
- Raise your arms above your head; your shoulders should be soft try and your biceps to your ears.
- Slightly turn your left foot behind you about 90 degrees, to face the wall on the left. See if your left foot heel, when moved sideways, is in line with the heel of your right foot.
- Lengthen up through the tip of your crown, reaching high through the fingertips.
- Maintain your hips in a square position, aligned with the floor and continue to breathe slowly.
- Repeat with alternate leg in front

Virabhadrasana II

- Begin the same as Virabhadrasana I, in a mountain pose.
- Inhale, and then as you begin to exhale, move your left leg behind you by sliding your left foot about four feet back.
- Bend your right knee as you do this, so you look as though you are lunging. Front knee should be stacked over the front ankle.
- Press the heels and big toe of both feet into the floor.
- The left heel and right heel should be in one line.
- Pull you navel towards your spine.
- Raise your arms to your shoulder height, with your left arm extended behind you and your right arm in front.
- Look straight in front, along the length of your extended right arm.
- Reach through to the end of your fingertips
- Breathe
- Repeat with alternate leg in front

Adho Mukha Svanasana

- In an inverted V shape, bend down and touch the floor with your arms, hands should width apart, feet hip width apart.
- Lift your hips and tailbone up and back
- Press the heels to the ground.
- Lengthen through the spine, drawing your navel towards the spine.
- Move your chest closer to your legs. You may not be able to plant your feet entirely on the ground if your hamstrings are tight, but that is okay.
- Breathe

Balasana

- Kneel, making sure to touch your big toes together and sit back on your heels.
- Gently stretch your upper body, as you bend forward, lengthening your tailbone towards the heels.
- Stretch your arms out in front of you, pressing your hands into the ground and fingers pointing forward.
- Touch your forehead to the floor or your yoga mat and rest your stomach on your thighs.
- Breathe

Shwasa

- Lie on the ground on your back. Loosen your feet and let them fall to either side.
- Your arms should be by your sides, but slightly spread away from your body with your palms facing up.
- Relax your entire body from your face to your toes.
- Elongate your neck, soften skin across the forehead, gently close your eyes, let your hips become heavy, and relax your legs.
- This will most often be the last pose in a yoga class, hold or at least five to ten minutes beathing and relaxing.

MASSAGE THERAPY TO HEAL ANXIETY

People love to talk about spa days, where they can enjoy an aromatherapy massage that is so relaxing and leaves them feeling refreshed and rejuvenated.

Well, it's true, spa days are great —except that massage therapy works beyond healing and rejuvenating tired muscles. In fact, a good massage has the power to heal the mind. A mere one-hour massage has proven benefits of lowering your cortisol levels while increasing the levels of serotonin and dopamine (Field et al., 2005).

In addition to influencing hormones that alter your mood, massage therapy can help with releasing the tension in muscles, increasing your chances of enjoying a good night's sleep. Scheduling a weekly massage to get rid of your tension will be a good way to start feeling better about yourself physically. And when the physical self is happy, it is reflected in the mental self.

Here are some tried and tested massage therapies that have proven beneficial to people dealing with anxiety issues:

- Lymphatic drainage. This is your main circulatory system. Sadly, though, the lymphatic system is highly sensitive to stress, and when under the influence of cortisol for prolonged periods, the entire system is in danger of shutting down. When the lymphatic system is compromised, you experience both mental and physical symptoms such as constipation, bloating, and a disruption in the digestive system. Lymphatic drainage will help with the block that your stress has caused and get the circulatory system up and running.

- Cranial sacral therapy. This refers to a form of massage that works to relieve your body of both physical and mental stress. By applying gentle pressure to the central nervous system, cranial sacral therapy triggers the body's self-healing mechanism, which can get overloaded when dealing with anxiety. This treatment reaches both the exterior and interior points of your nervous system. Stresses of the mind manifest through the body, and cranial sacral therapy is a very effective form of treatment.

Your negative emotions that affect and burden your body tissue are given a chance to heal through the light massage manipulations.

- Reflexology. You may have heard about this treatment, which is very popular and quite often available at locations that offer foot massages. Reflexology refers to a type of therapy that puts slight pressure on a specific point in your body. Your feet are the main points, although the ears and hands, will be treated at times too.

The treatment works on the same lines as acupuncture and is even called "zone therapy" because it connects exterior zones to internal zones. This means the therapist can offer relief to internal organs connected to specific pressure points on the foot. The treatment style is different from massage, as it helps energize as well as relax. Its benefits include pain reduction from arthritis, stress headaches, and stimulation of the nervous system.

- Myofascial therapy. This therapy is known to release symptoms associated with anxiety, insomnia, and depression. Myofascial therapy can also help with physical symptoms of migraine headache and TMJ, which is a condition where the jawbone gets locked, and can sometimes be caused by anxiety.

During the treatment, your muscles will be gently massaged to release tension. Tension can cause muscles to shorten or constrict, resulting in pain, fatigue, and feelings of tightness.

- Reiki. This is a combination of light touch and meditation. The name in Japanese translates to "universal life force energy." The treatment encourages relaxation and is known to reduce stress. Reiki can be practiced at home.

The benefits of reiki include:

- Stress and anxiety reduction.
- Alleviating fatigue and increasing energy.

- Empowering positive thoughts and getting rid of negativity.
- Improved relaxation.

Just like meditation and tai chi, reiki works through a series of poses using your hands to apply gentle pressure to energy locations on your body. Each one offers a specific mental and physical benefit. You will find instructions online for practicing reiki in the comfort of your home. All you require is a quiet, undisturbed corner. If you prefer allowing a professional to take care of your treatment, you should be able to find centers offering this therapy in your area.

- Shiatsu. This is a relaxing technique that works on your well-being by reducing your levels of cortisol. This traditional gentle massage therapy comes from Japan and helps heal your whole being, based on the theory that your body and mind are connected. Regular practice of Shiatsu will increase serotonin levels, help lower blood pressure, and may even improve heart conditions.

The method works in the same way Chinese acupuncture does, which is by placing pressure on your acupressure points with fingers and hands. Continuous therapy helps to prolong the build-up of stress and offers a deep sense of relaxation.

Body Scan Exercise for Healing Mind and Body

This is a technique very similar to mindful meditation, except that it focuses on healing through both body and mind. The technique works through sensation and visualization, which together create an awareness of your body.

As you focus on each part of your body, try to contemplate

the tension there, and direct your mind to visualize the release of that tension.

Body scan therapy works through the mind-body connection. If you've had a particular hard day at work, you may notice the tension you feel in your mind is reflected in your shoulders as a tightness; you will become aware of that connection as you do the scan.

How to Practice Body Scan Exercise

- Get into position. Lying down is best. You can do the scan this way before going to bed. Or if you prefer, sit cross-legged, or in another comfortable position of your choice.
- Take a few deep breaths, expanding your belly, until your breathing slows. Focus on the rise and fall of your belly.
- Concentrate on your lower body, moving upward in a gradual sequence starting at your feet. Focus on your feet and linger over them; see if your mind catches any pain or stress there.
- Scan your entire body this way, moving upward. Where you feel tightness and pain, work on releasing that pressure by breathing through the tightness and visualizing your muscles releasing. Your pain may not be gone but by visualizing in your mind that the pain is gone, you are focusing on your mind-body connection for relief.

Practice this consistently and you will get better at focusing on very specific points of stress. In time, you will be able to alleviate some of the pain and stress in your body through mindfulness.

Progressive Muscle Therapy (PMT)

This is very similar to the body scan exercise and will provide you with similar benefits. To practice progressive muscle therapy, you should lie down similar to a body scan, and follow these steps:

- Relax your body and take a few deep breaths.
- Pull your toes back, hold for a count of five and let go. Push your toes out and hold for a count of five and let go.
- Concentrate on your calf muscles; feel them tense, hold it, and let go.
- Press your knees together, feel the pressure of them pressing against each other, hold them thus for a count of five, and let go.
- Clench the muscles in your thighs, hold, and release.
- Make a fist with your hands, tighten, and let go.
- Move to your arms, tense the muscles, and let go
- Clench your buttocks, hold, and unclench.
- Squeeze in your abdominal muscles and release.
- Inhale, expand your chest, hold, then release the breath.
- Pull your shoulders up to your ears, hold, and drop them.
- Press your lips together, hold, and release.
- Raise your eyebrows, hold, and let go.
- Squeeze your eyes shut, hold, and open them.

Each time you tense and release a muscle, feel how that part of your body relaxes. Imagine the tension melting away from you and getting absorbed into the ground or mattress below you. In the end, your body will feel light and relaxed.

Benefits of Body Scan and PMT

- Reduced inflammation, insomnia, stress, and fatigue.
- May improve blood pressure.
- Reduces back pain and neck pain.
- Reduces the occurrence of migraines.
- Eases joint stress.

BREATHING TECHNIQUES TO IMPROVE ANXIETY

We have explored breath meditation, which showed you how concentrating on your breathing and being aware of inhaling and exhaling can help you focus, and essentially distract your mind from your anxieties. Now, we will look at some popular breathing techniques used to reduce stress and anxiety.

Deep Breathing Techniques

Practice deep breathing by sitting in a quiet space. You can stand if you wish but choose a spot where you are undisturbed.

Start by taking deep breaths in, that fill your belly; feel it expand, and then hold your breath, and let go. What you are doing here is counteracting the shallow quick breathing you associate with panic attacks or sudden anxiety that takes over. You are telling your mind that everything is calm with your long-concentrated breaths.

To focus more on the above-mentioned contrast, try to activate your sympathetic nervous system. You can do this by visualizing a traumatic scenario; something that stresses you out. Notice your rapid increase in breathing, feel your chest rise, and fall into the anxiety.

Then, turn your attention to deep breathing. Take deep, long breaths, and feel your heartbeat slow down. Enjoy the sensation and continue to breathe slowly and steadily.

Points to Keep in Mind When Practicing Deep Breathing

Remember that you cannot expect immediate results or perfection at the start. Therefore, it is important to keep the following points in mind:

- Don't be hard on yourself. Although you may not succeed at first, don't give up. A technique that seems easy, requires a lot of practice to master before it starts working.
- Be mindful of every breath you take and become aware of how your body reacts to each one.
- Download an app or look for a tutorial video to help you, you master the technique.

There are many different breathing techniques that you can explore once you have mastered the art of deep breathing. Remember that this is also a cure for sudden bouts of anxiety that can be triggered at any time. With that in mind, before you investigate more complex forms of breathing, I suggest you master deep breathing so you can easily practice the technique anywhere at any time. It will be a useful tool to help you calm down, and to improve your concentration and focus on the positive.

Next, we will look at a very simple, but often overlooked tool in wellness—proper nourishment. Let me enlighten you on the benefits of eating simple, wholesome, and nourishing meals.

6

NOURISH YOUR BODY AND SOUL

"Let food be thy medicine, thy medicine shall be thy food."
—Hippocrates

The benefits of eating a healthy, balanced meal can never be replaced by supplements, pills, or any other miracle boosters out there. Your body needs basic nourishment to function at its optimum best and this has nothing to do with fancy or expensive meals.

In fact, eating for your well-being is probably one of the most inexpensive options out there when it comes to food. In this chapter, I will include the types of food that help boost your brain power, immunity, and feelings of satisfaction.

We'll also look at food types to avoid, foods that can elevate your anxiety, cause your stress levels to increase, and influence the secretion of hormones that aggravate your anxiety.

Making small adjustments in your diet and food choices will bring huge benefits.

First answer the following questions:

- On a scale of 1–10, rate your food choices. Be honest: How happy are you with what you are eating? Is the food you generally eat healthy for you, or are you making unhealthy choices?
- How do you feel about your current diet? Does it leave you satiated, or does it leave you hungry within short intervals of eating a meal? Do you feel energized or sluggish after a meal? Do you suffer from diabetes or any other blood sugar-related disease?

To help you keep track of your dietary health, I have included similar quizzes to help you gauge your eating habits and fix any harmful eating patterns you may possess.

It may be time to make simple dietary adjustments if your answers were not satisfactory.

Toward the end of this chapter, I will introduce you to the essential benefits of aromatherapy. An age-old practice that has been used in several holistic treatments, aromatherapy certainly is food for the mind, body, and soul.

DOES MY FOOD AFFECT MY MOOD

A balanced diet should offer you more than physical benefits. Food rich in omega-3 oils, for example, promotes brain health and helps with improved cognition skills. Your diet must improve how you feel, help you to think clearly, and energize your mind and body. Here are my best tips for achieving these goals.

Make Sure to Eat Regular Meals

When you starve for prolonged periods of time, your body

ceases to produce glucose, and as your muscles and organs continue to absorb the glucose already present in your bloodstream, glucose levels are depleted, and your body no longer has an energy source. From here, you start to feel dizzy, out of focus, and essentially in a slump. Making sure to eat a regular meal at proper intervals is important for preventing such occurrences.

- Make it a habit to start your day with a high protein breakfast.
- Eat healthy snacks in between meals—nuts, fruits, fresh or dried.
- Try to limit lunch and dinner to small portions, including plenty of protein, vegetables, minerals, and vitamin-rich food.
- Avoid high sugar and simple carb food, especially at night. Limit alcohol consumption or avoid it altogether when you can.

Eat the Right Foods

Keep in mind that eating the wrong foods will trigger a spike in your blood sugar and make you hungry much faster. Therefore, it is best to avoid too much of the following.

Avoid Simple Carbs

Food made with white flour, as well as white rice, soft drinks, and desserts with added sugars should be avoided. Such foods turn into blood sugar very quickly and metabolized too soon, leaving you hungry, dizzy, and potentially nursing a headache.

Good carbs include whole grains where the bran has not been removed, as well as brown rice, steel cut oats, sweet potatoes, vegetables, legumes, and pulses.

Eat Fiber-Rich Food

Try to include plenty of high-fiber foods in your diet, as dietary fiber takes longer to digest and leaves you feeling fuller and happier until your next meal.

Look After Your Gut

Your gut microbiome is responsible for close to 90% of your serotonin levels, therefore, focusing on gut health is very important for controlling your anxiety. Make sure your digestive system is functioning well by including fiber-rich food. These include things like legumes, pulses, vegetables, whole grains, bran, fruits eaten whole, brown rice, berries, etcetera.

The dietary fiber looks after gut health and feeds the good bacteria there. Include plenty of probiotics like yogurt, or sauerkraut in your diet to improve the health of your gut microbiome.

Eat the Right Fat

Foods high in omega-3 essential fatty acid such as fatty fish (especially cold water) like salmon, mackerel and tuna, nut and seeds like walnuts and chia seed, and plant oils such as flaxseed, are especially great options. Fortified foods, certain brands of eggs and yogurt are also good. The benefits of omega-3 for brain health and anxiety are amazing, with studies proving the benefits of omega-3 in reducing symptoms of clinical anxiety disorders (Correl, 2016).

Choose healthy fats for cooking. Vegetable seed oils should be avoided, as they are high in omega 6, too much of which can cause inflammation and cancers. Include coconut and avocado oil for cooking at high temperatures. In addition, olive oil for garnishes is advisable. It has a low smoke point and should not be heated too much.

Include Plenty of Protein

Protein is responsible for the build-up of amino acids in your body. Amino acids aid with hormone production and regulate how your brain processes your emotions and thoughts. Besides, proteins help with satiety more than fiber and will keep you feeling full for much longer.

- Eat foods containing protein for muscle strength too, including lean meat, chicken, eggs, legumes, nuts, beans, tofu, nut butter, dark green leafy vegetables, and other protein-rich food types.

Drink Plenty of Water

Your brain and other organs are composed of over 70% to 80% water, therefore, make sure to drink plenty to keep your organs well hydrated. Blood flow also relies on water to refresh itself, while your digestive system will fail to function properly without adequate water. The results from dehydration are constipation, tension headaches, and bodily aches and pains, all of which can add to your stress levels increasing, and your anxiety being triggered.

- Drink seven–eight glasses of water a day or more.
- Smoothies, berry-infused water, and even sparkling water can be added to the count.
- Carry a bottle of water whenever you go out to stay hydrated.

Get Your Daily Quota of Fruits and Vegetables

Have you heard about the five fruits and five vegetables a day theory? Well, it's true. Fresh or frozen vegetables and fruits are chock-full of nutrients, minerals, and vitamins. Snacking on fruits and vegetables, as well as on dry fruits, is a great way to stock up on the nutrition factor.

- Have a bowl of fruit as your kitchen centerpiece to make sure you eat them on passing.
- Include plenty of salads in your meals where you can have a variety of vegetables, fruits, and nuts.

Control Your Caffeine

As you know, caffeine is a stimulant that gives you a high at first, resulting in a mental and physical crash soon after. Your morning cup of coffee may not be avoidable, but you can try to avoid caffeine before bedtime to enjoy a restful night's sleep.

- Avoid products containing caffeine, such as chocolate, tea, coffee, as well as soft drinks.
- If you find avoiding your coffee tough, consider switching to a decaffeinated version, or green tea. You will soon notice that a few days without your standard, caffeinated cup of coffee is going to improve your mood and anxiety levels by quite a bit (Richards & Smith, 2015).

Food to Avoid When Dealing with Anxiety

Food that causes sudden blood sugar spikes is not popular on the anti-anxiety diet. These include added sugars, simple carbs, and soft drinks. As well, foods high in gluten can trigger anxiety symptoms.

- Sodas and energy drinks. Regular and diet soda both fall into this category. Sugary sodas often contain excessive amounts of sugar, while diet sodas and energy drinks usually contain excessive amounts of caffeine.

- Fruit juices. These are not the same as whole fruits, and once you take out the pulp, you lose the fiber, leaving you with just the high sugar juice.
- Added sugar foods. Large amounts of sugar in your bloodstream can trigger anxiety, irritability, and mood swings. Foods containing added sugars that you should strive to avoid include certain types of salad dressing, ketchup, pasta sauces, sweet breakfast cereals, processed foods, and ready-made desserts.
- Simple carbs. Anything made with white flour; pastries, doughnuts, pancakes, white bread toast.
- Glutinous food is a trigger for anxiety. Apart from the usual suspects which are cakes, candy, white bread, and so on; glutinous food should be avoided, including soy sauce and processed foods.

Food to Avoid When Taking Medication for Anxiety

Your doctor or your healthcare provider should be consulted about the type of food you must avoid if you are put on anxiety or antidepressant medication. As a general idea, here are some food types that react badly with varied medications:

- Fermented, pickled, or smoked food, as well as chocolate, caffeine, and tea. Some antidepressants contain a substance called "MAOI," which when exposed to a substance called "tyramine," becomes toxic and causes dangerously high spikes in blood pressure. Food that is left exposed to the elements can acquire high levels of tyramine, which occurs naturally.

- Curtail your salty food intake and any additional salt in the diet, as salt can increase lithium levels in your blood. In addition to salt, some lithium supplements prescribed for anxiety-related types of mania and depression disorders can also raise your lithium levels.

These lithium supplements influence the secretion of serotonin but using them should be done consciously by reducing your salt intake. Salt, as well, will make lithium levels rise further, thus increasing serotonin in your bloodstream to unnatural levels. Too much of the hormone puts you at risk of heart ailments and seizures, which can lead to life-threatening conditions.

- Grapefruit, whether whole or juiced, can interfere with enzymes and how they metabolize the medication you are taking.

Food That Can Reduce Anxiety

Improving your overall well-being through diet is one of the best methods for improving your mental and physical health. There are also some types of food identified to reduce symptoms or triggers for anxiety while being highly nutritious. These include:

- Fatty fish rich in omega-3 essential oils. As I mentioned before, omega-3 fatty acids aid cognitive functions and improve mental health. It is important to keep your omega-3 levels balanced because if you consume inadequate amounts, and you eat foods high in omega-6 fatty acids, you may create an imbalance. Additionally, too much omega-6 is harmful as well, as it may cause a variety of illnesses.

- Eggs. These are virtually a superfood. The egg yolk is high in vitamin D, which aids in the absorption of calcium. Eggs contain tryptophan, which is a protein that aids in the production of serotonin. Therefore, eggs give you the benefit of serotonin, thus offering you the added benefit of mood elevation, improved sleep, and memory.

- Brazil nuts. High in selenium, Brazil nuts may aid with reducing inflammation, which is often present among people dealing with anxiety disorders. Selenium is an antioxidant, which means it helps to balance free radicals; the particles that cause cell damage and lead to cancers. Also rich in selenium are mushrooms and soybeans.

- Dark chocolate. Chocolate containing higher than 50% cocoa solids. There are some interesting studies that show a 40% reduction in stress levels among people who consume dark chocolate (Al Sunni & Latif, 2014). Other claims are that the flavonoids in dark chocolate could bring down neuroinflammation, which can cause cell damage, as well as bringing down the high content of tryptophan, which helps with the secretion of serotonin—ultimately improving your mood.

- Turmeric. Curcumin, the main component of the spice, has been identified as reducing stress.

- Yogurt. Yogurt is a probiotic that feeds the good bacteria in your gut microbiome, where serotonin is made. Therefore, the food contributes to increased feelings of happiness.

- Green tea. This kind of tea is adored for its calming effects. It contains L-theanine, which is an amino acid known to relieve stress and anxiety. Green tea has been known for aiding in concentration and can also rev up your mood and leave you feeling energized.

The Benefits of Herbal Teas for Relieving

Herbal tea has been drunk across the world for centuries, offering curative powers to its consumers. This type of tea is defined by the steeping of any type of edible plant in hot water. It can be any part of the plant, from roots to flowers to leaves. Although called "tea," herbal teas are not related to the actual tea plant (Camellia sinensis). Let's look at the benefits of popular types of herbal teas.

Curative Powers of Herbal Teas

Herbal tea has many benefits apart from its calming and soothing properties. The curative benefits of herbal teas extend to physical cures, and indirectly help with stress relief and reduce anxiety by addressing the factors that trigger anxiety.

Some of the physical benefit's herbal tea may offer include the following:

- Anti-aging, because of its antioxidative properties, it prevents cell damage caused by free radicals.
- Improving digestion, is important, as gut health directly affects the secretion of hormones such as serotonin. Also, ailments as constipation often increase a person's anxiety levels.
- Detoxifying and helping to flush out toxins from your body. Flushing out harmful elements from your body helps your organs and digestive tract to function at their optimal best, extending to your overall mental and physical health.

- Bringing down inflammation markers, as antioxidant herbal tea will control free radicals in your body, helping to reduce symptoms of chronic inflammation.
- You will find the benefits of herbal teas by adopting the practice of drinking a cup or two daily. Some work well as a bedtime drink, while others are good to enjoy once you get home at the end of a long day. Either way, try to incorporate the habit of enjoying herbal tea into your daily routine and watch for the benefits.

Best Herbal Teas for Anxiety Relief

- Chamomile tea. Containing flavonoids, the tea possesses antioxidants and anti-inflammatory qualities, as well as the ability to lower anxiety. It is a popular bedtime drink, as it helps alleviate insomnia conditions in some people and helps with a good night's rest. Studies have found that prolonged use of chamomile tea can aid in reducing the symptoms of generalized anxiety (Mao et al., 2016).
- Peppermint tea. The herb is a cross between spearmint and mint and is most commonly used to treat digestive issues. Some research suggests the tea offers relief from stress and anxiety, frustrations, and even feelings of fatigue.
- Gotu kola. Centella asiatica, also called "Indian pennywort," is a popular herbal tea that is said to improve memory. Drinking Gotu kola tea could help ease fatigue and anxiety, and some believe it is a curative drink for easing symptoms of Alzheimer's.
- Valerian root. It is believed this herbal tea, made from the root of the valerian plant, can help ease anxiety

and sleep problems that crop up due to stress, to promote restful sleep.

- Lemon balm. Used against depression and anxiety, lemon balm is also a curative tea to help ease sleep disorders. The tea boosts Gamma-aminobutyric acid (GABA) neurotransmitters in the brain that induce a relaxing and calming effect.
- Lavender tea. This pleasantly fragrant herb is popular as a calming oil used in aromatherapy. But lavender, when drunk as a tea, can help with relieving symptoms of anxiety together with the relief of body pains and other calming properties.

SECRETS FOR ENJOYING GOOD SLEEP

Now that you have learned about the benefits of herbal teas that aid with a good night's sleep, let's look at the importance of a good night's sleep for relieving your anxiety.

The quality of your sleep reflects your overall health. Therefore, it is important you understand the link between the wellness of your mind and body alongside the quantity and quality of sleep you enjoy each night.

Insomnia and other sleep disorders often share a link with anxiety and stress disorders. Ruminative worry, which we discussed in Chapter 1, likely invades your thoughts as you get into bed and try to fall asleep. Playing back the day's stresses and then worrying about achieving your delayed return environment goals will quite often keep you tossing and turning all night, leaving you waking up irritable and very close to setting off your anxiety triggers.

Poor Sleep, Insomnia, and Anxiety—What's the Connection?

There are several studies linking insomnia to various anxiety disorders and PTSD. Studies have concluded that higher sleep reactivity is more prevalent in people dealing with anxiety-related issues. This means that your high-functioning anxiety has the possibility of placing you at risk of developing insomnia or some form of sleep disorder.

One of the main elements that lead to insomnia is a condition called "hyperarousal," which is linked to anxiety. Add to these elements your general feelings of dread and foreboding, and you start to stress over falling asleep even before your head hits the pillow. Those thoughts are only going to increase your worry threshold and keep you from enjoying a good night's sleep.

And so, even when you do fall asleep, are there times you wake up and find it impossible to fall back to sleep because all your worries and stresses came flooding back?

This kind of sleep disruption causes sleep fragmentation and disrupts the quality and quantity of your night's sleep. Excessive worry and stress before sleep may cause a disruption in your rapid eye movement or REM sleep, the time your mind starts calibrating your thoughts and memories and are reflected as very vivid dreams. Anxiety can influence those dreams to become nightmares, then causing fear and negative thoughts in your mind, which you may associate with going to sleep.

If you are struggling with sleep disorders and you find your lack of quality sleep is aggravating your anxiety, there is a bright side. There are several methods available for improving sleep. Also, let's not forget that anxiety disorders are highly curable, and you can, therefore, look forward to improved sleep along with an improvement of your anxiety condition when proper steps are taken to lessen symptoms of anxiety.

Techniques to Improve Your Sleep Quality

There are several methods used to improve the sleep quality

affected by anxiety. Medications, such as beta-blockers and anti-depressants, are sometimes prescribed to combat the symptoms of anxiety, but may not always treat the underlying condition.

Cognitive-behavioral therapy (CBT), as explained in Chapter 1, is a more effective method for curing the underlying causes of anxiety and could help with sleep disruptions and insomnia. The most effective method for fighting sleep disorders is to address the anxiety that is causing poor sleep or has developed because of poor sleep.

CBT is highly successful and will help some people deal with anxiety issues successfully, but may not alleviate insomnia in others, in which case, a course of treatment called CBT-I, is the next step and may be recommended.

Cognitive Behavioral Therapy-Insomnia (CBT-I) works by analyzing your memories, thoughts, and behavior, and exploring their effect on your sleep. A trained therapist will help you to figure out the concerns you harbor that have a direct impact on your sleep, thus helping you to talk about it and find a solution that makes those negative thoughts—that are blocking your ability to enjoy a restful sleep—obsolete. Once the negative thoughts are analyzed and their power over your mind is lost, you can begin to heal.

Better sleep techniques you can start using immediately are focused on acquiring healthy rest and sleep habits.

How to Build Healthy Rest and Sleep Habits

As you deal with high-functioning anxiety, you may also be battling poor sleep quality, where your anxieties prevent you from settling down and enjoying the luxury of a restful night's sleep. You end up tossing and turning in bed all night, and you keep willing yourself to fall asleep, but it never works.

Have you tried getting your mind ready for sleep?

Here are some simple tips that will help you to set the right atmosphere, create the right vibe, and tell your mind that it is time to settle down and get some much-needed sleep.

• Your bedroom must be designed for sleep and nothing else.

Your laptop and anything else related to work does not belong in the bedroom. Your bedroom is not your pre-bedtime office, nor is it a place to watch a movie or even read a book. I highly recommend these activities be conducted in any other room but your bedroom.

Turn your bedroom into a serene cove designed only for sleep. Invest in a good mattress and pillow and get the best you can afford. An uninterrupted night's sleep will be well worth the extra cost if you suffer from insomnia. Make sure the room is uncluttered. Focus on dimmed lighting and muted colors for the wall. Blackout curtains will help keep outside lights from filtering in. Melatonin, the hormone that regulates sleep, is influenced by light, so having a brightly lit room will reduce the secretion of the hormone which inhibits sleep. Your room must be associated with sleep and not any other activity that is related to your stress.

• Create a quiet atmosphere.

Filter outside noise as much as possible. If it is beyond your control, try blocking noise pollution out by wearing headphones and listening to soothing music, playing white noise, or even wearing ear plugs.

• Adopt a regular sleep-wake cycle.

Go to bed at the same time and wake up at the same time each day. By doing so, you are fine-tuning your circadian rhythm to follow a pattern, and by training your biological clock, you are training your mind and body to follow a clear pattern of sleep and wake. Try not to sleep in for more than half an hour, even on weekends, to keep your circadian rhythm going.

• Don't be overly generous with your naps.

Naps should not be taken two–three hours before bedtime. And when you take one, limit it to 25–30 minutes maximum. The best nap times are in the early afternoon hours, after lunch.

• Change your sleep schedules gradually.

There will be times when your commitments require a change in your schedule, including your sleep-wake times. Once you know this fact for certain, start your transition early. If you require to wake up two hours earlier than your usual schedule, start by waking up half an hour earlier, then an hour, and gradually bump it up to two hours. This will allow your biological clock to adjust gradually, as a sudden change in your sleeping schedule can cause sleep disruptions, which will take longer to adapt to, and may aggravate your anxiety condition.

• Use aromatherapy to induce restfulness.

Aromatherapy oils used in a room scent diffuser works to soothe your senses and create a relaxed vibe within your mind.

• Create a wind-down zone in your house.

Get your mind ready for bed with subtle cues. An hour or two before bedtime, you can dim the lights in the house. This will get your melatonin secretion going and your mind will start preparing for sleep.

• Avoid blue light an hour before bed.

Blue light badly affects melatonin secretion. Your TV, laptop, smartphone, and tablet are all devices that emit strong blue light. Therefore, avoid the use of them at least an hour before your bedtime.

• Do not engage in vigorous exercises pre-bedtime.

It is recommended that you leave at least two hours between exercising and going to bed. Exercising stimulates your adrenaline and increases anxiety.

• Practice techniques to help you relax.

Meditation and a few yoga postures that stretch the body are very good stimulants for creating a calm, relaxed vibe within your body and mind.

• Turn to the soothing and comforting effects of aromatherapy.

Aromatherapy is so popular that it is presented in a variety of mediums. You can light scented candles, burn fragrant oils, pour a few drops on your pulse points, use it in a rejuvenating massage, and even spray your room with aromatic perfume to induce a good night's sleep.

Aromatherapy has many cures. From the soothing effects of lavender to the uplifting properties of peppermint and orange, the oils and scents may help your anxiety to a great extent. Therefore, pay particular attention to the next heading, in which we explore aromatherapy's powerful effects.

THE EFFECTS OF AROMATHERAPY AS A HOLISTIC CURING AID FOR ANXIETY

Aromatherapy works by activating aromatic phytochemicals in plant extracts to activate smell receptors in your nose. Aromatic phytochemicals refer to plant chemicals that offer a medicinal or soothing effect for healing and rejuvenating the mind, body, and soul. As the oils represent the essence and fragrance of the plant, it is called "essential oil."

Such extracts, when converted into essential aromatic oils, offer relief from anxiety and aid with sleep problems. Others may offer natural cures for symptoms such as sinusitis, indigestion, and inflammation.

How Are Essential Oils Made and How Do They Work

Essential oils are extracted from different parts of a plant. They can be derived from herbs, flowers, petals, as well as bark, roots, and peels from trees. The aromatic phytochemicals extracted from the plants are what you use for aromatherapy purposes.

Essential oils can be costly because it takes a lot of plant products to create a very small amount of oil. For example, only one pound of lavender oil can be extracted from two hundred pounds of lavender leaves. Also, some essential oils are not 100% plant extracts and will contain a chemical carrier oil, to which a percentage of the aromatic oil is added. If you don't mind splurging for a 100% oil extract, make sure to read the labels to ensure you are getting an undiluted essential oil.

Aromatic oils work by activating your sensors through smell or the application of the oil on your skin. Once the aromatic phytochemicals activate the smell receptors in your nose, your brain receives a signal stimulating certain systems; the hypothalamus, which manages your hormone secretion (including your serotonin levels), and the limbic system, which influences your behavior. These are believed to be some of the areas that get influenced by the fragrance in aromatic oils. The sense of calm and relaxation you experience from aromatherapy is possibly attributed to this stimulation of key receptors in your brain.

Benefits of Aromatherapy

Studies are not conclusive about the full range of benefits aromatic oils offer, so they should not be used in replacement of your regular medical treatment. It is believed that aromatic oils offer the following health benefits:

- Improve the quality of your sleep by activating your mood receptors.
- Help to soothe headaches and joint pains.
- Reduce feelings of stress, restlessness, and anxiety.
- Soothe sore joints or reduce pain in them.
- Uplift the mood.
- Guard or fight against certain types of bacteria or fungal growths, especially when you rub the essential oils on your skin.
- May help reduce side effects of chemotherapy such as feelings of nausea.
- May help with digestive problems.

Although not conclusive, aromatherapy is believed to help with some of the following medical conditions:

- Arthritis
- Insomnia
- Asthma
- Inflammation

- Depression
- Tiredness or fatigue
- Alopecia or hair loss
- Menstrual pains or other connected issues
- Menopausal symptoms

How Safe Are Essential Oils

Essential oils are natural plant extracts and are relatively safe. However, there are some people who could harbor allergies to some oils and will have allergic reactions, such as irritation of the mucous membrane, skin, and eyes. Also, essential oils are not regulated by the American Food and Drug Administration (FDA).

However, essential oils have been around for centuries, and skilled aromatherapists know about their safe use and benefits. Therefore, if you have never used aromatherapy, my advice is for you to find a reputed aromatherapist in your area and book a consultation. Once you are cleared of allergies and you know the types of oils that work to soothe your anxiety, you can choose to enjoy the benefits of the oils on offer at home.

How to Use Essential Oils at Home

There are several ways to enjoy the benefits of aromatic oils. These include:

- Aromatic sprays or spritzers you can used to scent rooms or to remove unpleasant odors.
- A diffuser is a good investment if you plan to enjoy the benefits of aromatherapy in your bedroom. A diffuser works by distilling water vapor to which a few drops of essential oil have been added.

- Bath salts infused with essential oils are another good method for relaxing and treating your skin and sensory glands with aromatherapy.
- Oils, lotions, and creams infused with aromatic oils will help your skin to directly absorb the oils.
- Compresses that can be used hot or cold for soothing symptoms of cold, sinus issues, or skin inflammations.

There are some studies that prove the positive effects of continuous use of aromatic oils to help relieve symptoms of anxiety, stress, and worry (Seo, 2009), especially among students studying for difficult exams and people dealing with long-term illnesses. Let's look at a few popular methods for using aromatherapy at home:

- Oil burners, diffusers, or cotton balls. Apart from using the oil burners and diffusers to release the aroma of the fragrant oils in your home, you can place a few drops of your favorite essential oil on cotton balls and place them around your home, allowing the rooms to be gently scented.
- In the bathtub. Enjoy the soothing benefits of a few drops of essential oils in your bathwater.
- Aromatherapy bracelets and necklaces can be used to have the soothing smell of the essential oils close to you when you go out. You can also try adding a few drops of oil to a facial tissue to inhale whenever you feel worried or anxious.
- Essential oils in a massage. Once you have identified the essential oil that works for you, consider using it in a massage. To do so, just add a few drops of the oil to a carrier oil, which is a base oil in which the essential oils are diluted. Popular carrier oils include

sweet almond oil, olive oil, jojoba, cold-pressed coconut oil, and apricot kernel oil.

The amount of essential oil you add to the carrier oil is very minimal, as the oil is extremely concentrated and should be no more than 1.5% to 3% of essential oil to every 10ml of carrier oil. Keep in mind that some essential oils are stronger than others and should be well diluted before rubbing on your skin, especially your face. The dilution ratio for massaging your face with essential oils is 0.2% to no more than 1.5% to every 10 ml of the carrier oil.

Most Popular Essential Oils That Help with Anxiety

Ancient holistic treatments have been used for centuries, although studies are inconclusive to confirm the effects of the oils. While I believe in the benefits some essential oils may offer people dealing with anxiety, I recommend you start using aromatherapy under the recommendation of your doctor, as well as with the supervision and advice of a qualified aromatherapist.

- Frankincense. This oil is used as a sedative and to help soothe anxiety. A good mood enhancer, Frankincense oil can sometimes be dabbed on points of the body, minus a carrier oil when you need it to work as a sedative.
- Ylang Ylang. It is believed that inhaling the essential oil works as a sedative and could reduce blood pressure while helping to deal with anxiety and depression.
- Rose. Rose oil helps you to deal with tension associated with being nervous. It also boosts self-esteem.

- Geranium. This oil also works as a sedative and helps to deal with nervousness and worry associated with depression and anxiety issues.
- Lavender. Especially helpful for insomnia and other sleep disorders, lavender oil helps to calm and still feelings of panic and depression.
- Bergamot. This final oil helps you deal with many symptoms associated with anxiety disorders, depression, nervousness, and insomnia.

As you become familiar with essential oils, you will find there are many others that can be used to ease anxiety symptoms. Once again, for safety reasons, check with your doctor or an aromatherapist before using any of the above oils.

Next, we will look at successfully managing your lifestyle, because managing your physical health only becomes 100% successful once you pair it with a well-organized and relaxed lifestyle. Chaotic schedules and stressful goals are only going to add to the weight of the burden your mind already bears. With that in mind, let's look at how you can lighten that load and manifest happiness and peace into your life through effectively managing your daily routines, commitments, and schedules.

7

MANAGING YOUR LIFE EFFECTIVELY

"We must first unpack our commitments, evaluate each one, and make a decision: keep the non-negotiable and that which matters most, and then toss the excess." —Emily Ley

A re you constantly overwhelmed; finding the day gets away from you before you have completed all the tasks you wanted, or are committed to fulfilling?

Do you stay awake at night worrying about the demands of your job, your responsibilities, promises, schedules, and your life in general?

Let's learn about taking control of your life to stop feeling overwhelmed, nervous, and flustered all the time. After all, these are the basic ingredients for creating panic, worry, and anxiety.

This chapter is dedicated to helping you overcome all those unwarranted worries. The things that keep getting in your way, whether it's the meeting at noon sharp, errands and housework you've got to finish before then, or that project you're not even halfway through. Can you relate to similar stresses in your life?

I found out that there are simple tools for putting such

factors into perspective, as well as methods and habits that can help you to get organized and worry much less.

In this chapter, I will empower you with tips and techniques for maintaining an anxiety journal for therapeutic benefits, as well as for putting your thoughts, worries, and stresses into focus.

Time management techniques are included to help you schedule your daily commitments more responsibly and realistically; thus, relieving the constant stress your mind is under.

Included are successful solutions that you can incorporate into your busy routines to ease the burdens and the constant worry of not meeting deadlines and dealing with unhealthy levels of stress for a happier and positive outlook on life.

JOURNALING A SUCCESSFUL TOOL FOR MANAGING ANXIETY

Did you keep a diary when you were young; a journal where you jotted down the day's events and then added your reactions, thoughts, and emotions?

A journal becomes your own mental health therapist, where you are free to express your worries, fears, sadness, and vulnerabilities—things you may not feel free to discuss with anyone. Journaling is a method that works for many people dealing with anxiety-related syndromes, with some studies even proving the effectiveness of journaling in reducing stress, worry, and an overall improvement in one's mental state (Smyth et al., 2018).

Journaling is one of the most private channels for admitting and dealing with high-functioning anxiety, which can be very well hidden by the sufferer.

Therapeutic Benefits of Journaling

Journaling is not a task. You are not required to diligently write down your day's experiences. I understand that for many, sitting down to write in a book is an additional chore that adds to their busy schedules, plus you may not like writing to begin with. That is why the type of journaling I am suggesting you do is flexible.

You are not required to record your thoughts and emotions daily; maintaining a journal with intermittent entries works just as well. Plus, writing in a diary is not a requirement, you can use any medium and any form that works for you. A word document on your computer, cue cards, or even on a doodle pad will work because, with these options, you can choose to type, write, or abstract-write. An example of abstract-writing could be writing a word, circling it, and connecting it to any emotions, or drawing—or even pasting—a memento of the day's events that caused you anxiety (a ticket stub, for example, to remind you of the movie that hit too close to home and made you realize a few things about yourself). Make it a fun and relaxing tool you use to help your emotional state and reap the following benefits.

Journaling Helps Put Your Emotions and Thoughts in Order

Dealing with confusing emotions and feelings becomes easier when you record them. This is a therapeutic method where you literally take those difficult thoughts and feelings out of your head and put them down in a medium you can look at and analyze.

Doing so creates a better awareness of exactly what you are dealing with and helps you form a proper perception of those emotions and what caused them. Quite often, you may end up recalibrating the type of emotion you associated with that event once you gain a proper perception of the entire event.

It Prevents You from Letting a Difficult Emotion Take over your Mood

Do you often allow a difficult situation and the stressful emotions it evokes, to keep interrupting your thoughts and processes?

The constant interruption causes you to brood over the event until it becomes a virus, at which point it takes over your mental state, making you very unhappy and distressed in the process.

Journaling stops you from brooding because writing about the event breaks the cycle of continuous worry. As a result, although you have not confided your emotions and thoughts to anyone else, you have placed them in a journal, thus putting them out of your head. That is a very freeing state of mental healing.

Make sure to write about the incident and or emotion a day or two after it takes place, as writing about it immediately after it happens will tend to aggravate the emotions you are associating with that event.

Learn to Control Your Emotions

When you write or doodle about your feelings in an abstract form, it will help you better understand them and deal with them, thereby calming those emotions, and not letting them interfere with the task at hand.

For example, if you're stressed and anxious about your school exams, you could doodle the word "exams," and then you write the emotions you are having around that word, be they "stress," "worry," and other words that capture your anxiety about obtaining a good grade. In this way you are taking charge of your emotions by coping with the incessant anxiety they are causing that prevents you from studying successfully.

You Learn to Become Open About Your Emotional State

As is the norm for high-functioning anxiety, most people dealing with the syndrome do not acknowledge the mental anguish they are dealing with. When you maintain a journal, you become aware of your mental state and the stresses you are dealing with. It helps to put into perspective your emotional state, as well as your vulnerabilities, which may not be on a normal level—you may get overly distressed or anxious over mundane events which do not require such heightened emotions.

When you journal those emotions, it helps you to realize your state of mind and could also help you determine if you could benefit from professional help.

Journaling Reduces Depression and Anxiety and Improves Physical Healing

Expressive writing a few times a week has many benefits. Studies conducted among people dealing with ill health and their resulting anxiety showed that maintaining and updating a journal as little as three times a week helped reduce their levels of anxiety and stress, which allowed them to deal with their concerns and fears over time (Smyth, 2018).

Similar to healing your psychological state, journaling may help improve your physical state as well. It encourages a positive mind to reinforce physical healing among people dealing with illnesses that are stressful and challenging.

HOW TO MAINTAIN A JOURNAL AS A TOOL FOR FIGHTING ANXIETY

Focusing on your thoughts and emotions is an integral part of dealing with your anxiety and achieving positive mental health. To reap the benefits of writing in a journal, you need to focus on your negative emotions and find meaning in them—this means finding their causes and triggers.

Again, journaling should be a fun technique. You can express your emotions in any way you like, in whatever medium you are comfortable in; you can do this daily or weekly, according to your schedule. Here are some steps you can follow to determine what form of journaling is right for you:

1. Uninhibited Writing—Freewriting

This type of journaling is a no-holds-barred type of expressive writing where you write down any thoughts or feelings you may be harboring at the time. Simply express those negative emotions and thoughts; there is no need to be polite or politically correct. The writing is for you to express yourself, as well as to get a better understanding of what you are harboring in your mind so you can uncover the truths, reasons, and triggers behind your anxieties and stresses.

Guide to Freewriting

- Decide on the length of time you wish to write for. Set a goal, maybe 20–30 minutes to begin with.
- Write the uncut version of your thoughts and emotions. Don't stop to think. If you are angry—go ahead and express that anger. The *why, who,* and *what* that leads to your anxiety, panic, stress, and ruminative worry should all be added up. Do not stop

to correct yourself. This type of expression can take any form: writing, doodles, etcetera.

- Your grammar does not have to be perfect. The main objective is to get those unsettling thoughts out of your head and onto paper, a word document, a journal —whatever works.
- Stop writing once your time is up. However, if you finish before the set time, continue to jot down your feelings and thoughts that come to mind, which relate to the emotion that ignited your need to write.
- Read what you just wrote. This is a crucial factor, because as you re-read, you may start to see those thoughts, reasons, and triggers in a new light which could change your perspective. Or you may have a sudden insight about how to avoid triggering that strong emotion the next time.

For example, an individual who often triggers emotions of anger or self-doubt in you, has triggered those feelings. By entering those emotions into a journal and then reading your entries, you will begin to understand and see a pattern that connects that individual's comments with your mood alterations. You will see that avoiding such toxic people is the best way to ensure your mental health remains positive.

Whatever insights and sudden epiphanies you have with regards to what you just wrote, go ahead, and write those down too. Then, connect the dots and see where they lead, along with how you can explore and understand your thoughts better.

2. Journaling to Help You Rethink Your Anxiety Issues

This type of journaling will help you to get a grip on your incessant worries.

Step 1:

Choose a time frame of 15–20 minutes, or more if you are not sure about how to begin your writing.

Begin by writing or expressing your thoughts in a form that is comfortable for you. They do not have to be connected to the day's events. Write down the worries that are in your mind at that moment. The stresses that are hovering just above the surface are ready to turn into anxiety attacks with the slightest trigger.

Write vividly, doodle, or draw the things that are causing stress for you. They may be related to a current situation or worries about future events.

Make a list of all the worries and analyze them; think from an analytical angle and you will be able to identify your pattern of negative thoughts and emotions, as well as the pessimistic attitude that is causing you stress. Most likely, you will be dealing with 'habitual stress,' which is unjustified.

Once you make this discovery, strive to change your strain of thoughts as it is possible you are dealing with cognitive distortions and stress.

Cognitive distortions, take place when your mind is closed. They are thoughts that cause you to perceive reality inaccurately and are often negative. These narrow-minded conclusions end up causing you a great deal of stress.

Journaling is a good method for dealing with cognitive distortions because it broadens your thinking by helping you see the thoughts and emotions—the ones associated with your mood alterations and anxiety—from a different perspective than what you perceive in your mind.

Once you identify your trend of cognitive distortion, it is easy to spot your negative stress-inducing habits of thinking, and in time—by being conscious of this fact—you will be able to put a stop to negative thoughts.

Here are some examples of how cognitive distortions work to induce stress. Look for them when you start analyzing the list of fears you wrote:

- Emotionally reasoning a situation. When you do this, you come to your own negative conclusions based on your emotion, rather than logically analyzing the situation. This makes you an emotional reasoner.
- Creating stress. This type of worry and anxiety takes place when you tend to blame yourself or someone else for a problem. You voluntarily accept blame for a negative situation, even if it is not directly connected to you. Conversely, you may blame someone else for making you feel the negative emotions you are stressing over.
- Mislabeling. Are you constantly putting people into boxes? Have you added a label to yourself, as well? Have you awarded yourself the title of 'loser' or your co-worker as 'conceited'? In doing so, you are narrowing down your perception of people, including yourself, to see them in a very limited and negative light. This limits your interactions with people and stops you from reaching your full potential.
- By magnifying problems and jumping to conclusions, you arrive at a negative conclusion, and then look for a reason to justify it, ignoring any logical reasoning that might prove you wrong.
- You dread going to a party because you think everyone there will ignore you, but when you go, people interact with you. Yet, your mind will tell you this was not done because they wanted to speak with you, but simply as a polite gesture, justifying your original negative conclusion.

You may be able to identify more cognitive distortions you possess as you continue with your journaling.

Step 2:

Read what you have written and take time to analyze the thoughts, concerns, and worries you have put down.

Think clearly and try to look for a solution. Is there any way you could change how you do certain things, and how you feel and react to certain incidents? Or perhaps those worries won't have such a big impact on you, if they did occur.

Decide on the importance of the ruminative worry you are harboring about current or future events over which you have no control.

How important are they? Are they worth the anxiety you are enduring? Quite often, you will discover that those worries are baseless and will not have a huge impact on you.

Step 3:

Give yourself more credit.

Instead of focusing on the negative, think about your strengths. Because although your mind keeps putting you down, you must have special moments where you were successful in life and achieved goals. Write those moments down so you can prove to yourself that you have more self-worth than you give yourself credit for.

Step 4:

Reassure yourself and reduce the level of fear-induced stress you are dealing with.

You can do this by formulating a backup plan in case fear does take place. Think about ways to deal with the problem.

That way you are deflating the fear of the unknown, which can be highly stressful.

Write down your backup plan against the fear you listed. It does not have to be foolproof but should be enough to avoid dealing with the immediate dread and stress by clearing your mind of the present worry you are enduring.

Record Your Thoughts

Jotting down your thoughts in what one might call a "thought diary" is a therapeutic tool that many mental health caregivers adopt when practicing CBT. In this way, you can spot the moment when your thoughts change, and therefore, you will be able to measure your progress toward avoiding cognitive distortions that cause stress.

Try the following format to easily maintain track of your thoughts:

Situation	Connected Emotion	What I am Thinking	Cognitive Distortion	The Logical Solution
In this column you write about the situation that caused your disturbing thought.	Write down the emotion you are dealing with because of the situation.	What are you thinking because of what transpired? Write down the actual thought and fear associated with the situation. If it was an argument, do you fear reprisal? Or maybe a missed deadline at work makes you think you are no longer getting considered for the promotion. Write down the fear and stress you are thinking about.	Think about and write down your thoughts on how realistic you think your fears and stresses are. Maybe you overreacted to losing your promotion because of a small slip-up. Or perhaps the argument wasn't as serious as you have made it out to be in your mind. Be critical and analyze that thought in a logical manner.	Try to find a more logical solution to the problem once you realize that your fear is unfounded. You're panicking about not getting promoted because you think your slip-up made you look bad, although no one mentioned it interfered with your promotion. What then would be the logical solution for you checking on the progress of your promotion?

Maintain a thought diary in this format. Adding the columns together will help you get a clear picture of what thoughts and emotions you associated with a particular event.

As the trend changes, you can also see how your pattern of thinking changes, thereby tracking your progress or even regression you may be making.

Moreover, a thought diary should be a tool you use to build resilience against worry, stress, and anxiety issues. The more you learn about your thoughts, emotions, and behavior, the easier it becomes to take control and see through the illusional thinking patterns created by anxiety.

Some Tips for Writing About Your Feelings

Not everyone is a writer, and I realize you may dislike

writing simply because the ideas don't flow. That is natural; we all have different strengths and weaknesses. Try these tips to overcome a writing block.

Write About Your Present Fears. It is better to express your negative emotions, rather than to suppress them in your mind where they fester and grow into more complex anxiety issues. Start by writing what you are feeling at that moment. If a certain event prompted you to write down your thoughts, start with that emotion.

It can even be one word: "Anger!"

You can write the word and then wait for the emotions to come crashing down. These could be emotions you associate with feeling angry—frustrated, or worthless.

Then, analyze those fears and look for ways to turn them around to your advantage. Write down the positive outcome you can gain from those emotions. If it is anger, for example, you can decide to use that emotion to become stronger.

ANGER = Don't be a pushover + Next time say 'no' + Avoid Alex, he makes me feel bad

Taking note of your most challenging feelings is the first step for opening up about your anxieties. Once you start, you will find that your inhibitions and vulnerabilities toward recording those emotions, thoughts, and ideas become easier.

Journal Prompt Ideas to Help You Get Started

Sometimes your thoughts can get stuck inside your head when you can't find the right means to express them. A prompt works by giving you a little hint to get you going. Here are some of the most popular and easiest prompts you can follow to get your writing started:

- I felt angry/sad when...
- Recently, I have been anxious about...
- Today was a positive day, and I am thankful for...
- What I love about myself is...
- The happiest memory I have is...
- My anxiety flares up when...
- My greatest accomplishments so far are...
- Maybe I judged the situation wrong; could it be that...
- I feel intimidated when I go out because...
- Dear Mom/Dad, I am writing this letter to tell you... (you can write the letter to either parent, without having to give it to them).
- What I would like to change about myself is...

Practice your expressive writing along the above lines, and as you become more fluent in jotting down your thoughts, you will be able to come up with more prompts you can use in your journal.

Together with your expressive writing, you must develop effective time management skills to try and develop the best coping mechanisms for your anxiety. Let me show you how to get started.

THE BENEFITS OF TIME MANAGEMENT TO BEAT ANXIETY

Time management is the backbone of our modern society, because how effectively you manage your time will have a direct impact on the amount of stress and anxiety you end up dealing with.

When you're trying to fit all your daily activities and obligations into a limited amount of time, managing an anxiety disorder can become even more challenging. Anxiety symptom flare-ups cause frequent panic attacks, mood alterations, and feelings of irritability; they disrupt and interfere with your relationships with your family and friends.

Ineffective time management, which makes your daily tasks pile up, will lead to extreme worry, on top of the ruminative worry you are already struggling with. Poor time management can also lead to additional triggers for the panic attacks, as you realize the day is not long enough to accomplish all your tasks. With that in mind, there are techniques you can adopt to manage your day better.

Effective Time Management Techniques

Time management techniques can reduce your stress by lessening the panic you feel every time your to-do list is left unchecked at the end of the day.

Keep in mind, that there may be unexpected factors that occur throughout the day to stop you from achieving everything you set out to do. Those unexpected events are beyond your control—understand that and strive to make the day as productive as it can be, instead of aiming for 100% success.

Techniques to Manage Your Day Better

- Make a realistic list, and schedule of how to achieve your day's tasks.

Forget the to-do list. Instead, make a list of what you plan to achieve with the day, and how.

By planning your day's schedule in this way, you are already looking for ways to accomplish your chores, which makes the list more realistic, since you will be able to determine how much you can accomplish. When scheduling, be very reasonable with the type of tasks and time frames you allocate to each.

Try not to add two or three tasks within the same time frame thinking you can juggle events around easily; those types of plans can fall flat the moment unexpected events crop up to throw a wrench in the works.

Plan less for the day so that you will be successful, rather than adding a medley of events into your schedule and struggling to get them done.

Here are some techniques you can try out:

- Avoid procrastination.

I know that anxiety often leads to procrastination in connection with tasks you are uncomfortable about getting done.

Avoidance will not make the tasks go away. They will still pop up the next day to make you even more anxious and stressed out. Therefore, when making your realistic list of daily tasks, add the difficult ones first and get them done. Prioritize by order of importance and not by the chores you like.

- Make a part of the day about yourself.

You will need time to recalibrate each day to soothe and calm stresses, emotions, and thoughts. You need time to practice your meditation, update your journal, and simply relax your mind, body, and soul. These are all important factors for managing your anxiety.

Schedule a small portion of the day for yourself. Trying to stretch your day by adding various chores and tasks until bedtime will only leave you exhausted, burned out, and on the verge of heightened anxiety, which could set off a whole string of symptoms.

By using the techniques, I have shared, you will be able to reduce the amount of pressure you feel as you attempt to accomplish all your tasks in a day. You will notice an overall improvement in your mood and less irritability when you are able to manage your day's tasks successfully.

These are not magic techniques that act as an excuse for you to load your schedule. Instead, each one is meant to show you the benefit of being realistic and true to yourself regarding the number of tasks you can handle mentally and physically.

Allocating time for you to recharge each day should be a priority. Following such methods will not only help with managing your anxiety and helping you feel relaxed and calm at the end of the day but will increase your productivity in the long run.

How to Write Easy to Follow To-Do Lists

Successfully manage your day and stop feeling overwhelmed by trying out some of the to-do list suggestions listed here.

Become a "List-o-maniac"

Okay, so a list-o-maniac is a fun word to help you find the humorous side of having several lists, in addition to the therapeutic value.

Making more than one list has many benefits because within a single day you are juggling more than one role.

You are part of a team at the office, a parent and or spouse at home, a caregiver to your parents, secretary to your youth club, student body president, etcetera. the number of roles we play within a day are numerous. Therefore, you need lists of to-do tasks that stand apart from each of these roles.

For example, if you make one list each for work and home, you will find that while completing the tasks you have written down for the office, you are reminded of the chores you must complete at home. You don't need that type of additional stress tumbling over the other.

So, go ahead and make any number of lists, keeping each one separate from the role you play. Keep your day's activities simple, prioritizing what needs to be accomplished just for that day; the rest you can simply reschedule for another.

Here are some ideas that may help you with creating realistic to-do lists:

- Office list. This refers to important tasks at work from one to ten (begin with one and then decide to reschedule those at the end if you do not have the time to complete them that day).
- Grocery shopping list.
- Chores list. A list of what you plan to complete at home.
- My weekend list. Tasks and events you want to leave for the weekend.
- My future goals list. This one is a predictive and motivational list of things you plan to achieve in the future. It is a fun method to keep you grounded and focused on where you want to be, or what you want to achieve in the future.

Prioritize and Add Deadlines

Not every task needs a due date but adding one to certain tasks can help you to prioritize, avoid procrastination, and manage your time excellently.

If you are using an app, assigning a due date means you can add reminders to keep you aware of your commitments.

Be Realistic with the Number of Tasks You Add to the List

You can add ten tasks to your list, but when you plan a realistic approach to achieving those tasks, you are going to find that the day is not long enough to do so. Hence, be smart and make your to-do list no more than four or five tasks a day. Try even less if the tasks are going to take long for you to complete.

Add Only Tasks to Your To-Do List

A to-do list is current and must therefore contain tasks you need to achieve daily. While you can make several lists to suit the different roles you play, make sure to keep the lists simple by not adding any objectives or goals. Objectives are the outcome of your goals, which are long-term plans, and therefore do not belong on your to-do list. Keep it simple.

Repeatedly Check Your List and Tick the Completed Tasks

Make it a habit to look at the list regularly, to guide you as the day moves along. Start by scanning your tasks first thing in the morning and mentally preparing yourself for what you must get done. Quick checks during lunchtime and closer to the evening will help you to stay on track and check off the completed tasks, leaving you with a happy sense of accomplishment before your scheduled 'me time.'

Simple Tool for Prioritizing Tasks on Your To-Do List

You should prioritize your tasks by importance and plan for the most urgent tasks to be completed first thing in the morning.

Sometimes, however, it may be difficult to know which tasks to prioritize when you have a group of equally important chores you need to get done.

Let me introduce you to the Q2 Matrix, which is a popular

tool designed for time management that many people use to help them decide on which tasks to get done first.

This is how your Q2 Matrix must look, with four quadrangles (Q1, Q2, Q3, Q4):

	Urgent	Not Urgent
Important	Q1	Q2
Not important	Q3	Q4

How the Q2 Matrix Works

- Q1 is the Quadrant of Necessity.

The task listed in this section are the ones you need to do as part of your job or lifestyle—they are necessary. They may not hold much importance in achieving your goals, but they are those daily tasks that guarantee your job and lifestyle are intact. These generally come with deadlines and time frames—your basic daily chores at home and the office.

- Q2 is the Quadrant of Extraordinary Productivity.

These are the activities that take you closer to achieving your goals. As they are mostly long-term plans, and are not considered urgent, but remain important. Put tasks on your list that will help you reach your goals - while setting aside time for you to relax and plan for the future - as well as those that cultivate important relationships.

- Q3 is your Quadrant of Distraction.

Here's where you look at those tasks in a realistic manner.

Add the tasks that looked urgent, but on proper analysis, turn out to be not so important after all. Most likely, you will take these out of Q1 after a proper evaluation and add to Q3.

For example, an advertising brainstorming session whose purpose is to sell a brand for a customer you are only handling the financial side of will be a waste of your time, as it is not part of your day's duties. Sitting in on that meeting, which is more directed toward the creatives handling the account, will only make you lose time that you could use productively back in the finance department. The task may be urgent, but not for you.

- Q4 is your Quadrant of Waste.

This means none of the activities you add here are important or urgent—keep them to a minimum. Dedicate the day to what you have in Q2.

Tasks that you would typically add in Q4 are those leisure time activities that are not productive or encouraging. If you have a favourite TV series you love to watch, but you end up binge-watching an entire season in one sitting while neglecting the rest of your day's tasks. That wasteful act belongs in Q4.

However, if you had just watched one episode to relax, and then turned off the television, the task then belongs in Q2 because relaxation improves your productivity.

Designating Tasks to Each Quadrant

Let's look at how you can use the Q2 Matrix to your advantage and allocate tasks on your to-do list in a realistic manner:

- The most important quadrant is Q2. Add as many tasks there as you realistically can; focus on self-healing, rejuvenation, and motivation.

151

- Q1, the Quadrant of Necessity, should contain only what is necessary as your commitments dictate. Keep the tasks there to a minimum.
- Try to add nothing or just what you simply cannot avoid to Q3 and Q4. Those are tasks that are counterproductive and will only take up your time.

Creating a Time Matrix of Your Own

1. Draw out a diagram as shown above and mark the quadrants and priorities as shown.

2. Add your tasks according to the parameters into each quadrant and make your to-do list.

3. Take one task from Q2 (extraordinary productivity) and add it to the top of your to-do list. The rest you can make up with tasks from Q1 (the necessity tasks).

The Q2 tasks are the most beneficial for managing your anxiety, but sadly, we often push back Q2 tasks to focus more on the necessary Q1 tasks, while even wasting time on Q4 tasks. When you put a Q2 task at the top of the list, you must make sure you complete that task before moving on to your committed tasks in Q1. Prioritizing Q2 tasks is prioritizing your mental and physical health—taking care of what really matters.

4. Tasks that you are uncertain about and cannot define by importance should be added to Q3 or Q4. Basically, these are distractions and counterproductive and may lead to later anxiety and panic, such as binge-watching television and worrying about missing your work deadline.

Tasks That You Can Add to Q2—Quadrant of Extraordinary Productivity

Dealing with the challenges of an anxiety syndrome such as high-functioning anxiety is all about learning self-worth, taking time to decompress, and dispelling ruminative worries. Here are some ideas on the type of tasks you can add to your Q2 list to heal your mental anguish and enjoy doing the things you love:

- Take time off to heal yourself mentally

We often need time away from everyone to recalibrate our thoughts, decompress, and rid our minds of the mental anguish that has built up.

When you feel the need to do so, do not let guilt or your commitments hold you back from enjoying some alone time. Prioritize your mental health; re-organize your tasks, complete the ones that cannot wait, and reschedule the others.

Avoid feeling guilty about taking care of your needs for a change. If you are worried about taking time away from your family, add those thoughts and emotions to your journal and analyze the basis of your guilt.

Is it realistic?

Does taking some time off for yourself affect your family as much as pushing your anxiety, and experiencing stress attacks?

Weigh the pros and cons, and you will see that your guilt is baseless. Talk to your family and explain the need for you to rejuvenate mentally and physically and see where they can offer support and give you strength.

Schedule some 'me-time' at least twice a week and encourage your partner to do the same.

- It is okay to say "no"

You are not required to be at everyone's beck and call all the time. Constantly putting other people's needs before yours, leads to a loss of self-worth and a build-up of stress and anxiety.

It is time for you to understand that at certain times, you are allowed to say "no"'—even to your family.

You must prioritize your needs and don't let anything deter you from achieving them; not even a friend who needs you immediately because she broke up with her boyfriend, or your spouse who needs you to iron a shirt just as you are about to take a long hot bath, or that work colleague who wants you to take over his shift on Friday because he has a date.

As you try to please everyone while putting your needs on the back burner, you are unknowingly building up your anxiety, which will reflect through your mood and irritability levels and end in destructive anxiety or stress attacks. You don't have to feel guilty about saying "no."

- Maintain a work-life balance

Ensure a healthy work-life balance for optimum mental health and job satisfaction. Do not make it a habit to work late every evening; make it clear to your employer that you are practicing your right to leave at the end of the working day. Working late and coming back more stressed the next day is counterproductive. Use the time management skills you have learned to complete your day's tasks on time.

- No need to be on a schedule all the time

Break free from the habit of thinking you need to be engaged in some task or another all the time. It is not a requirement, nor is it expected of you. Allocate a day to enjoy your own company and spend time reflecting on your life goals and achievements.

Alternatively, you could just find a quiet spot and simply

breathe and be aware of your surroundings and not think about anything.

Enjoy time alone doing nothing on your lunch break. Choose a few days to eat your lunch alone. Savor the food and your own company. Put away the devices and give yourself time to self-reflect.

How to Create the Right Ambience and Temperament in Your Life

Here is my last piece of advice on time management and getting your life organized to enjoy a calmer, more settled lifestyle that is a boon to your healing process. These are some simple tweaks you can make for maximum enjoyment of life.

- Get organized by scheduling and setting time frames for all your days and weeks activities. Set goals and work toward them; do not let your anxiety rule and deter you from achieving your dreams.
- Do not turn your brain into a diary. Instead, write down everything that you need to remember. Once you jot down your reminders, you are freeing your mind from keeping track of those tasks.
- Declutter and organize your home regularly because a clean and neat environment is easy on the mind, while chaotic surroundings can be distracting and unsettling. Consistently declutter your space by making sure your home does not become a storage unit for things you no longer need or use. When decluttering, organize your belongings so that everything fits into a designated space.

Creating serene and well-organized living spaces this way is very therapeutic for people dealing with anxiety disorders. You do not end up dealing with stressful situations where you get agitated looking for stuff, nor are you weighed down with constantly having to clean and re-organize your cluttered spaces.

As we come to the last chapter, let me introduce you to animal-assisted therapy, which is an alternative therapy showing promise for mental and physical healing, despite not being mainline.

8

ANIMAL THERAPY—
ALTERNATIVE STRATEGIES FOR
HEALING ANXIETY

"Until one has loved an animal, a part of one's soul remains unawakened." —Anatole Franc (McConnell, 2017)

Animal therapy is one of the more popular types of alternative therapies because pets have a knack for reaching our hearts and becoming a part of our lives, giving us purpose and a sense of belonging in the process.

The healing strategies I will discuss in this chapter are not mainline therapies that you will have heard of as popular healing methods, rather, they are simple strategies that have shown plenty of promise in easing anxiety-related symptoms.

WHAT IS ANIMAL THERAPY

The use of animals to help people dealing with mental health conditions and battling physical ailments is called "pet therapy," "animal therapy," or "animal assisted therapy." Specially trained therapy animals can perform a range of tasks that go beyond the therapeutic comfort they provide. They are trained to assist, warn others of dangers their charges may face, and provide physical and emotional comfort when needed.

Forming a bond with an animal is often easier and comes more naturally for people dealing with anxiety issues, as it triggers the natural human-animal bond we possess. Unless you have a very strong aversion to animals, there is nothing stopping you from forming a bond with a pet of your choice. Here are some of the benefits you can enjoy:

- Avoid being an introvert hiding at home because you will be busy enjoying walks in the park and active play with your pet.
- You can avoid bouts of boredom with a pet around.
- Socialization becomes easier when meeting other pet owners when you're out and about.
- Reduce your loneliness, as you enjoy the companionship and unconditional love of your pet.
- See a marked improvement in your character, your mood, and your overall outlook toward life.

Animal Therapy Helps Heal Anxiety—Scientific Claims on Animal Assisted Mental and Physical Healing

Animal assisted therapy has a few scientifically backed claims to prove there is an enhancement in a person's mental and physical health. Studies compound the healing power of loving a pet among people battling not only anxiety and depression, but also certain terminal and chronic illnesses.

- Petting and the release of feel-good hormones

There is science-backed research to show that petting animals triggers the release of feel-good hormones oxytocin, prolactin, and serotonin. The combination of these hormones can have a positive effect on your mood, elevating your feelings of happiness and contentment.

• Alleviates feelings of loneliness. Many individuals battling anxiety disorders and depression are struggling with loneliness. The thought of returning to an empty home at the end of the day is depressing. A pet can change all that, through the genuine and natural love it will show to their returning master. That welcome alone is enough to trigger a flood of positive emotions in anyone battling loneliness.

• Reduces your anxiety levels and helps you to calm down and stress less. With a pet around, you won't have time to sit and worry—or even feel sorry for yourself.

• Having a pet is a great comfort because of the unconditional love you receive.

• Pets provide plenty of distractions to deter you from wallowing in self-pity and can be the catalyst that makes your therapy a success by stopping you from being negative about the therapy and resisting the healing techniques on offer. A pet makes you want to heal and becomes a part of your overall well-being.

• Pets can help increase mental awareness in their masters and may have a positive impact on degenerative diseases such as Alzheimer's, amnesia, and even traumatic memory loss caused by head injuries.

• Benefits of animal-assisted therapy when dealing with autistic children, heart patients, dementia, and those in the ICU are positive, according to scientific research conducted in those fields (Animal.assisted.therapy, n.d.).

- Heart patients showed a reduction in blood pressure, improved lung function, and reduced levels of stress-induced anxiety after spending just 12 minutes with the therapy dog.
- Anxiety scores showed a 24% drop after the visit.
- Left artery pressure dropped 10% with the dog's visit.
- There was an impressive drop in the baseline anxiety score among the patients who spent time with the therapy dog as opposed to the group of patients who did not.

- Overall reduction of detrimental physical symptoms among patients.

- Reduces pain
- Helps calm laborious breathing
- Animal-assisted therapy motivated the patients to perform better and enjoy their therapeutic exercise sessions with more positive effects.
- Children with autism responded better and formed stronger bonds with the therapy dog than they did with people. They became more socially acceptable and engaged better with the therapist during the animal assisted treatment sessions.

What if I Can't Own a Pet

There are several reasons why people cannot own a pet, despite loving the concept. If you are in a similar situation, here are some suggestions for you to access animals to reap the benefits listed previously.

Become a Volunteer at a Local Animal Shelter

Your local animal shelter will certainly welcome an extra pair of caring hands to take care of their residents. Look up your local Animal Shelter and become a volunteer. Shelters are always looking for dog walkers and volunteers to interact with the cats waiting for their forever home. It's all very rewarding and you'll soon develop a purpose and look forward to going out and being a part of a team.

Check Out the Local Animal Shows

Scour the newspapers and notices online to find out where they are hosting animal shows. Dogs, birds, farm animals, and even reptiles are often put on display by their proud owners. Exploring a local animal show can be lots of fun, as you experience the love and bond between the animals and their owners and enjoy the antics of the animals there. Such distractions are ideal for lowering your stress and worries.

Become a Foster Pet Owner

Look for a local foster care program where you can care for animals, such as dogs and cats, until they are permanently adopted. However, if you feel that you may form too strong a bond that could trigger your anxiety once the animal leaves, this may not be the ideal option for you.

Join a College Veterinary Camp

Such camps are run by colleges offering veterinary degrees and are similar to the vet camps conducted at the zoo. They are ideal for college students, especially if you feel you need a break from your study program.

Spend Time at a Cat Cafe

Look for one in your neighborhood and enjoy relaxing with a good meal and a lazy kitty on your lap.

The power of unconditional love animals offer is unfathomable and looking for ways to ease your anxieties with the aid of a pet may hold the secret to your healing process becoming a success.

CONCLUSION

ANXIETY IS A HIGHLY TREATABLE DISEASE

High-functioning anxiety may not be a clinically diagnosed condition, but the symptoms are real, the challenges are difficult, and the road to recovery is long. However, there is light at the end of your journey. You now have the power to help yourself to overcome your negative thoughts, emotions, and behaviors by using the tools, techniques, and self-confidence you have acquired.

Make use of the unconventional methods I have described throughout this book and feel empowered to challenge your syndrome and fight your difficulties. Developing resilience and a strong will is the foundation for fighting your high-functioning anxiety.

Make a resolve to live a healthier, more fulfilling life, as procrastination is no longer a trait you possess. Embrace the fact that you are stronger than panic, stress, and anxiety.

Use your journal to take a deeper look at yourself. Don't hold back as you enter your deepest, darkest thoughts, and emotions—get them out of your head to get them out of your life.

Dare to dream big. You deserve the best in life. Turn your back on the fears, the dread, and the self-doubt by using the resources I've provided you with.

Be the person you are hiding under all that anxiety.

Break free and live your life free from anxiety!

Please Leave a Review

If you found my book helpful, informative, and a tool for changing your life, I would love to hear from you. Please let me know by leaving a review—Thank you!

Subscribe to my newsletter and receive a free downloadable copy of the companion workbook journal, Your Thoughts, Body, and Behavior a Healing Guide, visit me at www.cardeasirona.com

REFERENCES

105 Anxiety Quotes to Keep You Calm When You Feel Stressed Out. (2020, August 9). Happier Human. https://www.happierhuman.com/anxiety-quotes/

13 Celebrities with Anxiety Disorders | Everyday Health. (2018, November 12). EverydayHealth.com. https://www.everydayhealth.com/anxiety-pictures/celebrities-with-anxiety-disorders.aspx

54 Inspirational Yoga Quotes (Ready for Social Media Sharing). (2019, December 11). Seattle Yoga News. https://seattleyoganews.com/inspirational-yoga-quotes/

Acosta, K. (2021, October 14). *High-Functioning Anxiety: What It Is, Symptoms And Treatment.* Forbes Health. https://www.forbes.com/health/mind/what-is-high-functioning-anxiety/

ADAA. (2021, April 21). *Facts & statistics.* ADAA. https://adaa.org/under standing-anxiety/facts-statistics

Al Sunni, A., & Latif, R. (2014). Effects of chocolate intake on Perceived Stress; a Controlled Clinical Study. *International Journal of Health Sciences, 8*(4), 393–401. https://www.ncbi.nlm.nih.gov/pmc/articles/PMC4350893/

American Osteopathic Association. (2018). *Benefits of Yoga | American Osteo-pathic Association.* American Osteopathic Association. https://osteopathic.org/what-is-osteopathic-medicine/benefits-of-yoga/

Animal.Assisted.Therapy. (n.d.). *Animal-Assisted Therapy Research | UCLA Health.* Www.uclahealth.org. https://www.uclahealth.org/pac/animal-assisted-therapy#:~:text=For%20Mental%20Health%3A&text=Lowers%20anxiety%20and%20helps%20people

Anxiety Quotes (1629 quotes). (2010). Goodreads.com. https://www.goodreads.com/quotes/tag/anxiety

Anxious Depression. (2021, December 27). *What You Need to Know About Anxious Depression?* BrainsWay. https://www.brainsway.com/knowledge-center/anxious-depression-what-you-need-to-know/

Benisek, A. (2020, July 26). *Depression and Anxiety: Are They Hereditary?* WebMD. https://www.webmd.com/depression/are-depression-anxiety-hereditary

Berndt, V., Götz, E., Schönleben, K., & Langhans, P. (1978). [Stress-induced peptic ulcer; pathogenesis, clinical features, prevention and treatment (author's transl)]. *Praktische Anasthesie, Wiederbelebung Und Intensivtherapie, 13*(2), 108–122. https://pubmed.ncbi.nlm.nih.gov/652703/

Biswas, C. (2014, March 21). *20 Best Healthy Food Quotes To Inspire You.* STYLE-CRAZE. https://www.stylecraze.com/articles/slogans-on-healthy-food/

Black, D. S., & Slavich, G. M. (2016). Mindfulness meditation and the immune system: a systematic review of randomized controlled trials. *Annals of the New York Academy of Sciences, 1373*(1), 13–24. https://doi.org/10.1111/nyas.12998

Camille Noe Pagán. (2018, January 11). *What Is Aromatherapy?* WebMD; WebMD. https://www.webmd.com/balance/stress-management/aromatherapy-overview

Carpenter, S. (2012, September). That gut feeling. *Https://Www.apa.org.* https://www.apa.org/monitor/2012/09/gut-feeling

Cingulate Gyrus. (n.d.). Physiopedia. https://www.physio-pedia.com/Cingulate_Gyrus

Clear, J. (2016, March 22). *The Evolution of Anxiety: Why We Worry and What to Do About It.* James Clear. https://jamesclear.com/evolution-of-anxiety

Cleveland Clinic. (2020, April 19). *Thyroid Disease: Hypothyroidism & Hyperthyroidism | Cleveland Clinic.* Cleveland Clinic. https://my.clevelandclinic.org/health/diseases/8541-thyroid-disease

Correl, C. U. (2016, November 28). *Omega-3 fatty acids ineffective for psychosis in ultra-high risk adults*. Www.healio.com. https://www.healio.com/news/psychia try/20161128/omega3-fatty-acids-ineffective-for-psychosis-in-ultrahigh-risk-adults

Cronkleton, E. (2018, May 15). *Aromatherapy Uses and Benefits*. Healthline; Healthline Media. https://www.healthline.com/health/what-is-aromatherapy#conditions

Culpo, O. (2019, July 11). *Login • Instagram*. Www.instagram.com. https:// www.instagram.com/p/BzyOrV6nFrc/

Diagnosing Anxiety Disorders in Adults. (n.d.). Nyulangone.org. https://nyulan gone.org/conditions/anxiety-disorders-in-adults/diagnosis

Domes, Z. (2013, May 14). *How to Organize Your Life: 10 Habits of Really Orga- nized People*. Lifehack; Lifehack. https://www.lifehack.org/articles/productiv ity/how-organize-your-life-10-habits-really-organized-people.html

Drillinger, M. (2018, July 31). *The 5 Worst Foods for Your Anxiety*. Healthline. https://www.healthline.com/health/mental-health/surprising-foods-trigger-anxiety

Duffy, J. (2021, August 18). *Get More Done: Try These 10 Simple Tips for Better To- Do Lists*. PCMag UK. https://uk.pcmag.com/get-organized/127199/10-ways-to-make-better-to-do-lists

ESPN. (2018, August 21). *When making the NBA isn't a cure-all: Mental health and black athletes*. ESPN. https://www.espn.in/nba/story/_/id/24393541/ jackie-macmullan-complex-issue-mental-health-nba-african-american-community

Field, T., Hernandez-Reif, M., Diego, M., Schanberg, S., & Kuhn, C. (2005). Cortisol decreases and serotonin and dopamine increase following massage therapy. *The International Journal of Neuroscience, 115*(10), 1397–1413. https:// doi.org/10.1080/00207450590956459

REFERENCES

Flannery, S. (2018, April 23). *The Incredible Benefits of Massage for Anxiety*. Zeel. https://www.zeel.com/blog/massage/the-incredible-benefits-for-massage-on-anxiety/

Gerasimo, P. (2020, November 1). *Emotional Biochemistry*. Experience Life. https://experiencelife.lifetime.life/article/emotional-biochemistry/

Gialelis, J. (2018, September 11). *7 Massage Modalities to Reduce Anxiety and...* Massage Professionals Update; Institute for Integrative Healthcare Studies. https://www.integrativehealthcare.org/mt/massage-for-anxiety-and-depression/

Gonzalaz, R. B. (2020, January 14). *Manage Your Time to Help You Manage Your Anxiety | HealthyPlace*. Www.healthyplace.com. https://www.healthyplace.com/blogs/treatinganxiety/2020/1/manage-your-time-to-help-you-manage-your-anxiety-1

GoodTherapy.org. (2016, February 2). *7 Ways Anxiety Actually Works to Your Advantage*. GoodTherapy.org Therapy Blog. https://www.goodtherapy.org/blog/7-ways-anxiety-actually-works-to-your-advantage-0202165

Goodwin, R. D., Weinberger, A. H., Kim, J. H., Wu, M., & Galea, S. (2020). Trends in anxiety among adults in the United States, 2008–2018: Rapid increases among young adults. *Journal of Psychiatric Research, 130*(PMCID: PMC7441973), 441–446. https://doi.org/10.1016/j.jpsychires.2020.08.014 .

Grinwis, S. (2020, September 2). *30 Journal Prompts for Anxiety and Depression-Repost*. Medium. https://medium.com/@thesunshinesuitcase/30-journal-prompts-for-anxiety-and-depression-repost-1763b3d5ac01

Halber, D. (2018). *Motivation: Why You Do the Things You Do*. Brainfacts.org. https://www.brainfacts.org/Thinking-Sensing-and-Behaving/Learning-and-Memory/2018/Motivation-Why-You-Do-the-Things-You-Do-082818

Healingscents. (2018). *Healingscents*. Healingscents. https://healingscents.net/blogs/learn/18685859-history-of-essential-oils

Herbal Tea Benefits: 8 ways herbal tea benefits your health. (2019, May 18). The Times of India. https://timesofindia.indiatimes.com/life-style/food-news/8-ways-herbal-tea-benefits-your-health/photostory/69385326.cms

High-Functioning Anxiety. (n.d.). Bridges to Recovery. https://www.bridgestorecovery.com/high-functioning-anxiety/

Hirsch, C. R., & Mathews, A. (2012). A cognitive model of pathological worry. *Behaviour Research and Therapy, 50*(10), 636–646. https://doi.org/10.1016/j.brat.2012.06.007

Hofmann, S. G., & Hay, A. C. (2018). Rethinking avoidance: Toward a balanced approach to avoidance in treating anxiety disorders. *Journal of Anxiety Disorders, 55,* 14–21. https://doi.org/10.1016/j.janxdis.2018.03.004

Hohenhaus, D. A. (2019, January 30). *10 ways your family can enjoy animals without owning a pet.* The Animal Medical Center. https://www.amcny.org/2019/01/29/10-ways-your-family-can-enjoy-animals-without-owning-a-pet

Hull, M., & Crowley, D. C. (2022, May 26). *Identifying & Coping with Anxiety Triggers | The Recovery Village.* The Recovery Village Drug and Alcohol Rehab. https://www.therecoveryvillage.com/mental-health/anxiety/anxiety-triggers/

Iliades, C. (2018, January 5). *Photo Gallery: 7 Anxiety-Attack Triggers.* Everyday-Health.com. https://www.everydayhealth.com/anxiety-pictures/7-surprising-causes-of-anxiety.aspx

Is high-functioning anxiety really a thing? (2020, August 12). Citizen Advocates. https://citizenadvocates.net/blog/is-high-functioning-anxiety-really-a-thing/

Jarvey, N. (2020, January 15). *Social Media Influencers Struggle with Anxiety Amid Pressure to Create Perfectly Curated Feed.* The Hollywood Reporter. https://www.hollywoodreporter.com/lifestyle/lifestyle-news/social-media-influencers-struggle-anxiety-pressure-create-perfectly-curated-feed-1269805/

Johnson, J. (2020, July 10). *Animal therapy: How it works, benefits, and more.* Www.medicalnewstoday.com. https://www.medicalnewstoday.com/articles/animal-therapy#what-it-is

Kasala, E. R., Bodduluru, L. N., Maneti, Y., & Thipparaboina, R. (2014). Effect of meditation on neurophysiological changes in stress mediated depression. *Complementary Therapies in Clinical Practice, 20*(1), 74–80. https://doi.org/10.1016/j.ctcp.2013.10.001

Kiken, L. G., & Shook, N. J. (2014). Does mindfulness attenuate thoughts emphasizing negativity, but not positivity? *Journal of Research in Personality, 53*(PMID: 25284906), 22–30. https://doi.org/10.1016/j.jrp.2014.08.002

Lawson, K. (2013). *What Lifestyle Changes are Recommended for Anxiety and Depression? | Taking Charge of Your Health & Wellbeing.* Taking Charge of Your Health & Wellbeing. https://www.takingcharge.csh.umn.edu/what-lifestyle-changes-are-recommended-anxiety-and-depression

Leonard, J. (2021, May 28). *High-functioning anxiety: Definition, symptoms, signs, and more.* Www.medicalnewstoday.com. https://www.medicalnewstoday.com/articles/high-functioning-anxiety

Life Management Quotes (5 quotes). (2019). Goodreads.com. https://www.goodreads.com/quotes/tag/life-management

Lithium: Uses, Side Effects, Interactions, Dosage, and Warning. (2018). Webmd.com. https://www.webmd.com/vitamins/ai/ingredientmono-1065/lithium

Malzer, C. (2019, October 31). *How To Reach Enlightenment Through Body Scan Meditation.* The Conscious Club. https://theconsciousclub.com/articles/2019/10/17/body-scan-and-vipassana-reaching-enlightenment-through-the-physical-body

Mao, J. J., Xie, S. X., Keefe, J. R., Soeller, I., Li, Q. S., & Amsterdam, J. D. (2016). Long-term chamomile (Matricaria chamomilla L.) treatment for generalized anxiety disorder: A randomized clinical trial. *Phytomedicine, 23*(14), 1735–1742. https://doi.org/10.1016/j.phymed.2016.10.012

Mayo Clinic Staff. (2020, April 22). *A beginner's guide to meditation.* Mayo Clinic. https://www.mayoclinic.org/tests-procedures/meditation/in-depth/meditation/art-20045858

McConnell, S. (2017, April 6). *28 Inspirational Dog Quotes about Life and Love | PlayBarkRun*. Playbarkrun.com. https://www.playbarkrun.com/27-inspira tional-dog-quotes-life-love/

Medical Network, H. (2021, June). *25 Teas That Relieve Stress and Anxiety*. Healthline. https://www.healthline.com/health/anxiety/tea-for-anxiety

Mental Health Benefits of Journaling. (n.d.). WebMD. https://www.webmd.com/ mental-health/mental-health-benefits-of-journaling#:~:text=Journaling% 20about%20your%20feelings%20is

Mental Health Foundation. (2021). *Smoking and mental health*. Mental Health Foundation; Mental Health Foundation. https://www.mentalhealth.org.uk/a-to-z/s/smoking-and-mental-health

Milzoff, R. (2016, December 5). *Billboard Women In Music "Trailblazer" Kesha: My New Songs "Showcase My Vulnerabilities As a Strength, Not a Weakness."* Bill-board. https://www.billboard.com/music/awards/billboard-women-in-music-trailblazer-kesha-my-new-songs-7597386/

Miss Malini. (2021, May 7). *Check-in With Yourself by Asking These 6 Questions*. MissMalini | Latest Bollywood, Fashion, Beauty & Lifestyle News. https:// www.missmalini.com/2021/05/07/check-in-with-yourself-by-asking-these-6-questions

MTI, S. (2017, April 10). *Using the Cognitive Triangle to Combat Anxiety and Depression - Sinews Multilingual Therapy Institute*. SINEWS. https://www.sinews. es/en/using-the-cognitive-triangle-to-combat-anxiety-and-depression/

Murray, B. (2002, June). Writing to heal. *Https://Www.apa.org*. https://www. apa.org/monitor/jun02/writing

Newman, K. (2016). *Five science-backed strategies to build resilience*. Greater Good. https://greatergood.berkeley.edu/article/item/ five_science_backed_strategies_to_build_resilience

NIMH» I'm So Stressed Out! Fact Sheet. (n.d.). Www.nimh.nih.gov. Retrieved May 2021, from https://www.nimh.nih.gov/health/publications/so-stressed-out-fact-sheet

Nunez, K. (2020, August 10). *Progressive Muscle Relaxation: Benefits, How-To, Technique.* Healthline. https://www.healthline.com/health/progressive-muscle-relaxation#how-to-do-it

Panossian, A., & Wikman, G. (2010). Effects of Adaptogens on the Central Nervous System and the Molecular Mechanisms Associated with Their Stress—Protective Activity. *Pharmaceuticals, 3*(1), 188–224. https://doi.org/10.3390/ph3010188

Parade. (2020, February 1). *101 Anxiety Quotes to Help You Get Through and Lift Your Spirits.* Parade: Entertainment, Recipes, Health, Life, Holidays. https://parade.com/951718/parade/anxiety-quotes/

Pham, T. (2021, July 20). *How To Prioritize Todo Lists With A Sheet of Paper.* Asian Efficiency. https://www.asianefficiency.com/productivity/prioritize-todo-list/

Princing, M. (2018, June 4). *This Is Why Deep Breathing Makes You Feel so Chill.* Right as Rain by UW Medicine; RightAsRain. https://rightasrain.uwmedicine.org/mind/stress/why-deep-breathing-makes-you-feel-so-chill

Purse, M. (2021, March 30). *Techniques to Tame the Fight-or-Flight Response.* Verywell Mind. https://www.verywellmind.com/taming-the-fight-or-flight-response-378676

Raypole, C. (2020, May 28). *Daily Meditation: 7 Ways to Make It a Habit.* Healthline. https://www.healthline.com/health/daily-meditation#get-comfy

Reichenberg, A., Yirmiya, R., Schuld, A., Kraus, T., Haack, M., Morag, A., & Pollmächer, T. (2001). Cytokine-Associated Emotional and Cognitive Disturbances in Humans. *Archives of General Psychiatry, 58*(5), 445. https://doi.org/10.1001/archpsyc.58.5.445

Reiki Self-Treatment. (n.d.). Cleveland Clinic. https://my.clevelandclinic.org/health/treatments/21080-reiki-self-treatment

Ressler, K. J. (2010). Amygdala Activity, Fear, and Anxiety: Modulation by Stress. *Biological Psychiatry, 67*(12), 1117–1119. https://doi.org/10.1016/j.biopsych.2010.04.027

Richards, G., & Smith, A. (2015). Caffeine consumption and self-assessed stress, anxiety, and depression in secondary school children. *Journal of Psychopharmacology, 29*(12), 1236–1247. https://doi.org/10.1177/0269881115612404

Ritchie, H., Roser, M., & Dattani, S. (2018). *Mental health*. Our World in Data. https://ourworldindata.org/mental-health

Sachan, D. (2020, July 30). *It's Probably Time for a Self Check-in—Here's How to Do It*. Real Simple. https://www.realsimple.com/health/mind-mood/emotional-health/self-check-in

Saxon, S. (2022, May). *Avoidance Behavior: Examples, Impacts, & How to Overcome*. Choosing Therapy. https://www.choosingtherapy.com/avoidance-behavior/

Scott, E. (2021, March 31). *Journaling to Cope with Anxiety*. Verywell Mind. https://www.verywellmind.com/journaling-a-great-tool-for-coping-with-anxiety-3144672

Seo, J.-Y. (2009). The Effects of Aromatherapy on Stress and Stress Responses in Adolescents. *Journal of Korean Academy of Nursing, 39*(3), 357. https://doi.org/10.4040/jkan.2009.39.3.357

Serotonin Transporter Gene : CSHL DNA Learning Center. (n.d.). Dnalc.cshl.edu. https://dnalc.cshl.edu/view/862-Serotonin-Transporter-Gene.html

Serotonin: What Is It, Function & Levels. (2022, March 18). Cleveland Clinic. https://my.clevelandclinic.org/health/articles/22572-serotonin

Shah, S. (2020, December 11). *The 5 most common types of meditation — and how to choose the best type for you*. Insider. https://www.insider.com/guides/health/mental-health/types-of-meditation

REFERENCES

Shapland, K. (2022, February 9). *How Stress Affects the Lymph.* Legology. https://legology.co.uk/how-stress-affects-the-lymph/

Sharma, A. (2021, November 9). *What Is a Type A Personality?* WebMD. https://www.webmd.com/balance/what-is-a-type-a-personality

Shiatsu for Stress and Mental Health issues | Theale. (n.d.). Thealewellbeingcentre.co.uk. Retrieved June 3, 2022, from https://thealewellbeingcentre.co.uk/shiatsu-for-stress-and-mental-health-issues/

Smyth, J. M., Johnson, J. A., Auer, B. J., Lehman, E., Talamo, G., & Sciamanna, C. N. (2018). Online Positive Affect Journaling in the Improvement of Mental Distress and Well-Being in General Medical Patients with Elevated Anxiety Symptoms: A Preliminary Randomized Controlled Trial. *JMIR Mental Health, 5*(4), e11290. https://doi.org/10.2196/11290

Spitzer, D. R. L., Williams, D. J. B. W., & Kroenke, K. (1995). *Self-Test for Anxiety.* https://www.uofmhealth.org/sites/default/files/healthwise/media/pdf/hw/form_abn2339.pdf

staff. (2004, February 1). *Mind/Body Connection: How Emotions Affect Health.* Familydoctor.org. https://familydoctor.org/mindbody-connection-how-your-emotions-affect-your-health/#:~:text=Your%20body%20responds%20to%20the

Stress vs. Clinical Anxiety and How to Spot the Difference. (n.d.). Www.arnold-palmerhospital.com. https://www.arnoldpalmerhospital.com/content-hub/stress-vs-clinical-anxiety-and-how-to-spot-the-difference

Stuart, C. (2018, August 1). *9 foods that help reduce anxiety.* Www.medicalnewstoday.com. https://www.medicalnewstoday.com/articles/322652

Suni, E. (2020, July 30). *How to Sleep Better.* Sleep Foundation. https://www.sleepfoundation.org/sleep-hygiene/healthy-sleep-tips

Thorpe, M., & Link, R. (2020, October 27). *12 science-based benefits of meditation.* Healthline. https://www.healthline.com/nutrition/12-benefits-of-meditation

Thyroid disease: How does it affect your mood? (n.d.). Mayo Clinic. https://www.mayoclinic.org/diseases-conditions/hyperthyroidism/expert-answers/thyroid-disease/faq-20058228

Time. (2017). *Kesha: The Holidays Are Hard If You Struggle With Mental Illness.* Time. https://time.com/5041017/kesha-self-care-holidays/

Villines, Z. (2019, April 17). *Stress ulcer: Symptoms and treatments.* Www.medicalnewstoday.com. https://www.medicalnewstoday.com/articles/324990#causes

Vogue. (2018, June 4). *Ariana Grande Covers July Vogue.* British Vogue; British Vogue. https://www.vogue.co.uk/article/july-cover-vogue-2018

Waters, S. (2022, January 3). *10 ways to take time for yourself even with a hectic schedule.* Www.betterup.com. https://www.betterup.com/blog/take-time-for-yourself

Watkins, M. (2019). *Anxiety and Alcohol: How They Are Linked.* American Addiction Centers. https://americanaddictioncenters.org/alcoholism-treatment/anxiety

What is Myofascial Release and How Can it Help Me?: RehabOne Medical Group: Physical Medicine & Rehabilitation. (n.d.). Www.rehabone.com. Retrieved June 3, 2022, from https://www.rehabone.com/blog/what-is-myofascial-release-and-how-can-it-help-me

Wilkinson, L. (2017, April 18). *Craniosacral Therapy for Anxiety and Stress.* The Elbowroom. https://www.the-elbowroom.com/health-clinic/craniosacral-therapy-for-anxiety-and-depression/

Worry Management. (2019). https://www.talkplus.org.uk/downloads_folder/Worry_management.pdf

Zoldan, R. J. (2022, January 17). *7 Beginner Yoga Poses to Get Through Your First Class.* Life by Daily Burn. https://dailyburn.com/life/fitness/beginner-yoga-poses-positions/

ABOUT THE AUTHOR

Cardea Sirona has been an educator for over 18 years. Her greatest achievement is that moment in a student's eyes when she's made that connection and they 'get it'. However, Cardea's drive to excel led to struggles with anxiety and depression since her early 20s. It wasn't until she discovered the mind-body connection, and how it could help in her own healing, that she found an effective treatment.

Cardea has combined her love for teaching, and the techniques she discovered during her own healing journey to help others achieve the same successful outcome that she has. Her goal is to provide practical solutions to help those dealing with anxiety overcome their negative symptoms so that they too, can embrace a healthier and more enjoyable lifestyle.

An avid gardener, and beachcomber, Cardea is now living her best anxiety free life on the Oregon coast, doing what she loves with her family, and two rescue dogs Boris and Reva by her side.

Made in United States
Orlando, FL
21 December 2022

27437894R00104